CW00405605

SURVIVING DRUG ADDICTI

Confessions of a <u>Recovered</u> Drug Addict and Alcoholic

By Jack Llewellyn

Footprints

One night a man had a dream.

He dreamed he was walking along the beach with the
Lord. Across the sky flashed scenes from his life. For each
scene, he noticed two sets of footprints in the sand. One
belonged to him, and the other to the Lord.

When the last scene of his life flashed before him, he
looked back at the footprints in the sand.
He noticed that many times along the path of his life, there
was only one set of footprints.

He also noticed that it happened at the very lowest and
saddest times in his life. This really bothered him and he
questioned the Lord about it.:

"Lord, you said that once I decided to follow you, you'd
walk with me all the way. But I
have noticed that during the most troublesome times in my
life, there is only one set of footprints. I don't understand
why when I needed you the most
you would leave me."

The Lord replied, "My precious, precious child, I love
you and would never leave you.
During your times of trial and suffering, when you
see only one set of footprints, it was then I carried
you".

Author Unknown

Foreword

In the years since my recovery from alcoholism and drug addiction, which started over 34 years ago, I have come to realize that as a practicing alcoholic and drug addict I was a sick person, and that there was absolutely nothing I could have done to stop these killer addictions taking control of my life. The way they crept up on me and the nature of my downwardly spiraling behaviour were all part of the natural progress of my disease. Today I am aware of many others who have had the same experiences that I have, and many of them helped me to find the alcohol and drug free life that I have been blessed with today.

Where ever and whenever I took the first drink of the day, I had no idea what was going to be the result or where I would end up. Would I be arrested or hospitalized again? Would I blow what little money I had left on a prostitute or be in my bed or a strange bed with someone I did not remember meeting or ever seeing before? Or would I be alone with only the most horrendous hangover and all-consuming self-pity for company, not having a clue what I had done the night before? One or more of these was *always* what followed my taking the first drink of the day!

Since I became 40 and quit booze and drugs I have lived a life of such extraordinary diversity and happiness that it seems important for me to pass on my experiences to others, so that it may help them climb out of the self-made hell alcoholics and drug addicts create for themselves. "My way" eventually led to me living my life with an attitude of utter despair, wanting to be dead but not having the courage to take my own life. Today, it is not like that. I have found a life, lived mostly in bright sunshine, which has kept getting better as the years rolled by, sadly quicker now that I enjoy them so much.

***

Alcoholism and drug addiction are the cause of over 60% of crime, as well as massive amounts of mental and physical health problems: almost every country in the world suffers such results. In addition families and societies are often devastated by the mayhem both cause. Although the problems are easy to identify, due to a lack of understanding very little is done to remedy the basic issues.

As someone on the inside track with many years of recovery from both, I decided to write a book whose aim is to help others similarly addicted. I realized that even if it only helps one person recover from either addiction, the years of writing it and living in my past life's self-created hell will have been worth it, though my hope is it will help many, and the knock-on effects will be of much benefit to society in general.

Understanding alcoholism and drug addiction is not easy even when you are an alcoholic or drug addict. And if you are not, I would go so far as to say it is impossible. As the result of such misunderstanding, the stigma 'weak character' was attached to every alcoholic and drug addict before the middle of the last century. Today, the medical profession has a better understanding of drug addiction, believing that it applies to anyone who has a physical allergy as well as a mental craving for whatever chemical substance or substances they are addicted too: therefore it is an *illness,* and now recognized as such by the world's health authorities.

From my years as a 'junkie' who became addicted to almost every mood-altering chemical I took, I gradually came to believe this view to be true. From alcohol to cannabis, cocaine or 'crack' to heroin, LSD to ecstasy, tranquillizers to sleeping pills, 'uppers' to 'downers', antidepressants to 'magic mushrooms', purple hearts to glue, opium to morphine, nicotine to caffeine: I tried many of them and the result was instant addiction almost every time. This view was reinforced by the thousands of other addicted people I spoke with over the next 20 years who had become similarly hooked on whatever narcotic they took.

The knowledge that I was a sick person not a bad person meant that for the first time in my life I no longer felt isolated and different to everyone else on the planet. In time I gained hope for the future and became a well-balanced, worthwhile member of society: in other words I developed a love of life, the world's people and a realistic self-worth; I was restored to sanity.

****

God, "You may fool all of the people some of the time; You can even fool some of the people all of the time; but You can't fool all of the people all of the time" – especially alcoholics and drug addicts who have been smashed to smithereens and been put back together again!

Abraham   Lincoln   (Approximately!)

PART I – "DESCENT INTO HELL"

Chapter 1

THE MAKING OF AN ALCOHOLIC AND DRUG ADDICT

Where in hell am I? I cannot remember anything. I am lying on a floor on my side and all I can see around me are men's legs and bodies! I raise my gaze a little and I see bars. I gradually realise I am in a prison cell. Where am I? How long have I been here? And how did I get here? These are the questions running through my terrified mind.

My hangover is no different to the thousands of hangovers I have had in the past 25 years, but never had I found myself in such a position as this before. I continue to lie there, going through the events of the previous 24 hours as best I can remember them. I am in 'blackout', a condition I am very familiar with – unable to remember what I had done the night before!

I had started drinking at San Francisco's airport just before boarding my flight to Los Angeles. I drank more on the flight and more in Los Angeles on arrival. I had flown in from London two days before, and except for sleeping, I had been drinking and taking drugs around the clock.

I had an arrangement to stay with a woman who lived in Santa Barbara. I had assumed this was a suburb of Los Angeles and that she would meet me at the airport. Geographically speaking I was a long way out – Santa Barbara is a good distance from Los Angeles and she had meant she would meet me at the airport in Santa Barbara! By the time I met her I was in pretty bad shape.

It was early evening and she quickly appraised my condition. She said:

"You are acting very strangely. There is something seriously wrong with you".

I knew she was right and tried to laugh it off. When we had met in Spain a few months earlier we had established a common bond in relation to drugs, so I was quite surprised when she said:

"I am not having you to stay with me. You are far too sick and making me feel scared".

She dumped me at a motel and from that moment on I can hardly remember anything; though I vaguely remember falling down some steps and into a bar, also falling into some bushes when I thought I had seen a police car.

As I lay on the floor of the gaol, I realised I badly needed a *Valium* fix. I searched my pockets and found there was nothing in them. Usually I kept around 30 milligrams on me for such emergencies. I started to panic and got to my feet. I fully comprehended for the first time that I was in the biggest police cell I had ever been in and there were several other men in it with me. I went to the door and asked to see someone. Eventually someone came and I explained my situation; that I was a British citizen on holiday! None of the rest of what happened do I remember except that there was a lot of controversy about my not having a passport or any other means of identification, coupled with lots of talk of deportation!

It was decided that I would be taken by police car in search of my motel. As we drove off I turned around and read a huge sign, which said, *Santa Barbara State Penitentiary*. For the first time I knew where I was! We drove for several miles and proceeded to the area where presumably I had been picked up the night before. We eventually found the motel at which I had registered and
- fortunately for me - my passport, flight details and ticket home. It was suggested by the officers accompanying me

that I leave the country as soon as possible. I did not need telling twice.

* * *

By now the demon alcohol had me well and truly in its grip. Little did I realise that my dependency on it and other drugs was soon to cause me more misery than anything I could ever have imagined. It was already bad enough! But what had caused me to fall into this seemingly bottomless pit?

In my childhood I was described as a "likeable little boy". I had grown up in an honest, loving family, so how had I become a self-obsessed, dishonest and very frightened individual? One who had become an altogether unwanted, out of work member of society. What happened to cause this and why had it all crashed around me?

I was told alcoholism is often hereditary but there was no one in my family who had a drink or drug problem. One of my cousins had recreated our "family tree" going back over 150 years and had found only one distant relative who had such a problem. He was known as "Middle-of-the-Road" Tom, as that was where he always walked to avoid falling in the ditch! I discovered he had been a hangman's assistant – no wonder he drank, I thought.

I reflected on my childhood as I sought to answer the simple question: how had I become a chronic alcoholic and drug addict? I wondered, for example, where I had got my dishonest streak from. At home I was taught a high moral code for living. The trouble was I broke almost every one of the principles that my parents and teachers taught me in my early years. My way of living, lying and stealing led me to believe that I was a very bad person; and that my self-loathing was to continue to grow for many years to come. Again, as I looked back further, I recalled how I had been thrown out of both the Cubs and Boy Scouts. That sort of thing I knew did not happen to "nice little boys", so why, I wondered, had it happened to me?

I could not see that my troubles were all self-created and *never* of anyone else's making. It was all very well being cast aside by my friends, and blaming them for deserting me, but worst of all I had come to loathe myself. The moral code I had been taught in my youth I had shattered to smithereens - so much so, that as soon as I awoke every morning my first waking action was to put my hand under my bed seeking the prescribed tranquillizers I had left there the night before. I knew I would need them to help me over the depression I always immediately felt nowadays upon wakening. This feeling was exacerbated by the hangover from the previous day's alcohol and the fear of what I might have done! Once I had 'fixed' myself with the tranquillizers to combat this depression, and taken much liquid to deal with my dehydration, I was more or less ready to face the 'long' day, which I knew lay ahead of me.

In school, almost overnight, I had become known as 'Jack the One-balled Wonder'. This was when it was noticed by my schoolmates that only one of my testicles had dropped! I was extremely ashamed of my defect and my attitude toward it was to haunt me for many years to come.

For some extraordinary reason I decided to join the police cadets. The police medical examiner refused to take me unless I had the misplaced organ removed. He thought that I might get kicked in the misplaced testicle by someone and that would be the end of my manhood dreams! I never did understand his reasoning. My parents were all for it and, much to my shame, the operation to remove it was carried out shortly after. I realised that once it was gone, it was gone forever, and that I would, therefore, never ever fully be a man!

I told all this to my not too bright, first 'real' girlfriend, Sue - who unfortunately told her mother. Though she was only 17,

Mum did not think it a good idea for her daughter to get further involved with a man who may not be able to perform the manly duties of fatherhood later in life. I was 'madly in love' with Susan and argued that I was sure it would all be okay. Needless to say, Mother's will prevailed, and Sue went out of my life almost forever. The nails were being hammered, one by one, into the coffin of my lack of self-confidence.

Eighteen months later I was at the police training centre in Bridgend, South Wales. One of the regular pranks played on new recruits was 'black-balling'. This meant several men holding down a fellow trainee whilst colleagues rubbed black shoe polish onto the unfortunate suspect's testicles. I learned on the grapevine that it was my turn that night. I was horrified. I was mostly afraid of what my fellow trainee officers would think of me, and my *deformity*! I had never told any man of my operation, and now here I was, faced with everyone in the training camp knowing by tomorrow morning; that or telling the ringleader, Tony, and pleading with him to protect my dignity! I chose the latter course, and much to my surprise nothing happened - thank God! Whether he told others about my misfortune I never found out.

Shortly after Sue ditched me I started dating Mimi, a girl I had worked with for a few months. Mimi was attractive and "experienced". Also, she was very nice. I would dearly love to have had sex with her but as soon as the opportunity arose on the back seat of my car one night, *absolute terror* overcame me and that was the end of that. At about the same time, an old school friend Stella and I got into an identical 'back seat of my car' situation with the same dire results. Two more nails in my ego driven coffin.

I had many more similar excursions to the edge of full sex in the next five years but all proved as fruitless as those with Mimi and Stella. Whilst all my mates seemed to be having 'it' left, right and centre, I certainly was not. In fact the longer my virginity lasted the further away from 'it' I seemed to go and more afraid I got.

Due to the same physical *defect* therefore, at age 23, I was still a virgin. By then I was living in North London and had a girlfriend called Jennifer. Jen had the most infectious laugh I had ever heard and I adored her. We had dated for several weeks and were headed in a straight line towards my first ever full sexual encounter. Again I was terrified. What would happen when she found out? I decided to tell her. We had gone back to my place and were lying on the bed when I took the bull by the horns!

"Jen, there's something I have to tell you," I blurted out: "I've never had sex!! You know where other boys have two; I unfortunately only have one…" I stammered.

I expected her to sympathise and say something like, "Darling, it doesn't matter at all. I want you so much, just do it." Instead, she roared with laughter; so much so, that I actually joined her - though I have to admit, to a slightly lesser extent! Needless to say we never did make love, and our fling finished shortly after. From that moment on I never told anyone of my deformity, I just got drunk and drugged up to the eyeballs. They could take it or leave it – no one seemed to care, and towards the end, most of them did the latter!

It was already obvious to me that although unfortunate, only having one testicle had not made me an alcoholic. I thought back to my 'laziness'. Was that it? My mother had continually accused me of chronic slothfulness, "You are as useless as your father. If it goes on like this I am thinking of leaving." This was not a criticism of her, for I knew my laziness was a fact of life. After all, when I was supposed to be studying for my 'O' levels, almost all I did was sit in my study area listening to pop music, rushing to turn off the record player whenever I heard parental footsteps approaching!

I was also a rebel, was that the cause? Any time I was asked or told by anyone to do something I did not want to do, a huge resentment welled up inside me and I rebelled. I lived with my sister Marianne, Mother and Father. Marianne was six years older than me and seemed to revel in dishing out discipline to her 'much-loved' brother. I followed her through both primary and secondary schools, and I was always being compared to her in what seemed to me as a most derogatory manner. "You are not as nice as your sister You don't work as hard as your sister…" And so it went on for eleven very resentful years.

I could not understand it. I thought I was a loveable, intelligent, good-looking, pleasant boy who **never** did anything wrong, whereas she was a stupid, ugly, bossy cow! Why didn't **they** understand me better and see it my way?

An evening at home went something like this:

Me: "Let's watch Z Cars!"
Her: "No. I want to watch The Newcomers. Look, Mum, Jack's picking his nose again!" Me: (thinks): "I'd like to kill her!"

After supper:

Her: "Jack, it's your turn to do the washing-up." Me: "No it isn't, I did it last time!"
Her: "These plates are still dirty!"
Me: "No they're not, I just washed them!"
"If only someone else could have had my awful sister!" I thought.

Today I adore my sister and see that I am no lazier than anyone else – so that was not what made me a 'junkie' either. Years later I was to learn that **_resentment_** is the number one offender in alcoholics and drug addicts, with **_fear_** keeping up a good pace alongside. In the 1950's and

1960's pubs were still closed in Wales on Sundays. Every night except Sunday, at about 8.45pm, my father would say,

"I'm off to the pub now then, Kit." Kitty was my mother's nickname, which came from Kathleen, one of her several Christian names. My father was called Doug, adapted from his Christian name Edgar. I was named Jack because my mum and dad liked it. My second name, though, was Edgar, which I did not like at all – I knew of no other Edgars on the planet, so why me?

I used to wonder what my father did in 'the pub' *every night*. In later years, when I was old enough to join him, I discovered that all he did was drink about two pints of beer, play dominoes and sometimes darts or cribbage. How boring, I thought, and how I hated my first taste of best Welsh bitter, very flat, beer. Little did I know then this would become my way of life too, *but not just two pints of beer*! He would return home just after 10.30 p.m., when the pubs closed. I can recall how much safer the house felt with him back home – he would fight off any burglars, I thought.

When I was eleven or so, my sister went to live in Cardiff, the Welsh capital, and life got infinitely better! Around that time too, I passed my '11 plus' exam and went to the local grammar school in Llandrindod Wells. 'Llandod', as it was known, was the second largest town in the county of Radnorshire; the least densely populated county in England and Wales – less than 10,000 citizens but with enough sheep to impress any New Zealander – I was teased accordingly! It was 21 miles from where I lived in the village of Glasbury-on-Wye, and to get there I caught the school bus every morning at 7.45a.m. I would arrive home again about 5.00 p.m. I quickly learned to do the little homework I bothered to do on the bus, where I could copy freely from fellow my pupils. This left my evenings free to play with my friends.

Growing up in a village the size of Glasbury, with a population of approximately 500, was bliss for a child. Every night there were about eighteen of us who used to play on the village green, in the local woods or down by the river. Games of hopscotch, kick-tin, hide-and-seek, Cowboys and Indians, cricket and football were my daily habits until the aged of about fifteen. From sixteen my interests became gambling, pub games and girls!

I went to a 'mixed' school and travelled on a 'mixed' school bus. Because of this and the fact of having a sister I got used to girls quite quickly, *but* I was afraid of most of them. When I was twelve I had a crush on Ann. She was a year older than me and she quickly recognised my somewhat bashful advances aimed at her. One day she sent me a letter in French. It started, 'Est ce que vous adores moi?' I ran a mile!! I was terrified - what had I done? I was already having enough trouble with my mother and sister, and now this!

Shortly after, I completely flipped over Gillian. She was also a year older than me. She was tall, had a wonderful figure and long blonde hair. I worshipped her. Almost every day I sent her, via her girlfriends, sweets and chocolates. I could tell they were laughing at me but I did not care and knew that one day my amorous attentions would win her heart. I sent her love letters as well! The funny thing was that in five years of seeing her almost every day I never said a single word to her in all that time – I was overwhelmed with chronic fear!

The *big date* at the time was to go the pictures with your heart-throb. By now I had fallen for Josephine. She was adorable and I found out she liked me too; again I had not dared speak to her. We arranged, via some friends, to go to the cinema one Saturday afternoon. I was really looking forward to it. We were to meet outside at 2.55 p.m., five minutes before the picture started. I was more nervous than I had ever been in my life. I literally quivered from head to foot. At three minutes to three I could stand it no longer. I panicked, bought my ticket and went inside. It was very dark. About five minutes later she walked in on the other side of the cinema. I cowered in my seat and eventually crept out, hunching myself well below the level of the height of the seats. I was too much of a coward ever to tell what had happened. In the next three years I discovered Josephine was one of the nicest girls I would ever meet, and have always wished I had had the courage to tell her so. She died several years later aged just eighteen. Such a tragedy, I thought.

There were two very 'naughty' girls on the school bus, Belinda and Veronica. They were well 'into boys', along with Elvis, Buddy Holly, make-up and all that sort of hip thing. They were fun but I was afraid of them and as the result I felt 'very small' in their company: they were several years older than me as well. One day they persuaded me to sit with them. They had me sit on their knees and started to tease me in a nice kind of way. Suddenly I realised their hands were inside my trousers and they were about to grab me by the testicle and 'willy'! I was terrified and struggled to free myself. They were strong, and it was only by making a huge commotion that I was able to free myself – to me this was a matter of life and death! Yet another blow to my 'manliness', as I knew many of my mates would have enjoyed it and revelled in the attention.

At this time winkle-pickers were the *in* shoes and drainpipe trousers the *in* pants. Teddy boys were all the rage. My mother did not like Teddy Boys, the shoes or the pants! My best friend was Martin, he was allowed to wear something resembling both. Also he had a terrific 'DA' (ducks- arse!) type hairstyle. I had a really stupid *wave* my mother liked. At this time my face was covered in spots and blackheads. My mother and I tried every trick under the sun to remove them. But as quickly as we did, more would come and take their place. My sister said it was because I did not wash properly, which did not endear her to me anymore than she already was. So *I* also hated the way *I* looked and was dressed. Was there anything *I* liked about *me*? It certainly did not seem so but now I see that all *I* ever did think about was *myself*. **_Self-centredness_** I later learned was another distinguishing trademark of every alcoholic on earth. I now see I had 10 out of 10 junkie trademarks so far!

By the time I was sixteen I was starting to get seriously interested in a girl in my local village. I had doted on her for many years, since the age of about eight in junior school if I remember correctly. Her name was Diana. She was a few months older than me with beautiful jet-black hair, a permanent mischievous smile and mysterious, very dark eyes. She was seriously good- looking and as Rod Stewart said, "Every schoolboy's dream.". I found out she had taken up bell- ringing - campanology, to give it its proper name. Needless to say, I joined the local church bell- ringers. I would have followed her anywhere. We also became hand-bell ringers too, though this did not further my love notions and manoeuvrings either. We used to go from house to house at Christmas playing carols and collecting for the local church. (It turned out the vicar actually walked off with the funds – and was defrocked as the result!)

Then Paul Anka came out with the then most successful pop song ever, *Diana*. I used to listen to it for hours at a time. It actually was a great pop song, a classic in its own right. Unfortunately, the other Diana and I never did get together, and we went our separate ways: I on my journey of self-destruction and Diana to who knows where? I always knew I was fighting an uphill battle, as Diana had always preferred the company of her cousin Michael to me, and when *John* became ill he was feted with all her attention! But I liked a fight and did not give up easily; another aspect of my error-strewn, ***selfish*** life! And of course ***selfishness*** is another trait of those of us who take to chronic addiction, as we all always want our own way with everything and loathe it when we do not get it.

Saturday nights, by now, were spent at the local cinema in Hay-on-Wye (now the world famous second hand book shop!). There would be a 'B' movie followed by a more star-studded affair. By the time such films reached Hay, they were two or more years old, but that did not bother my friends and me. The stars were mostly Doris Day, Elizabeth Taylor, Jane Russell, Marilyn Monroe, Bridget Bardot (if we were lucky), Julie Christie (if we were very lucky), Humphrey Bogart, Robert Mitchum, John Wayne, Marlon Brando, Kirk Douglas, Dirk Bogart, Rock Hudson, David Niven and Paul Newman. I would catch the 6 o'clock bus with the Jones Brothers, Billy and David, plus their cousins Tommy and Johnny, to be there on time for the one showing that started at 7.30 p.m. Between the bus's arrival and the movie starting time we went to the local café. Coffee, one-armed bandits, a pinball machine and a juke box were the attractions here; plus of course the local 'crumpet'! I was too shy to make much progress in this department, but eventually my friends set up my first date!

Wendy was her name. I will never forget my first kiss. After half an hour of having my arm draped around her neck, or resting on the seat behind her, I made my move! I knew she was experienced and for her it must have been almost painful. I had no idea about 'French kissing' and just pushed my very closed mouth against hers, moved it around a bit and removed it. I did this three or four times before the film ended and that was that. We walked out of the cinema together, kissed tentatively 'good night' and off she went, never for me to date again. And I was left wondering what all the fuss around kissing was all about!

Then Johnny told me about Sexy Sam! I was terrified, but I had seen her several times at a distance and I liked what I saw. This was 'big time'. We were to meet near her place and walk to the cinema together. I had been carefully briefed on what she would let me do and not do. Needless to say, I was a miserable failure. Sam, though, did not seem to mind and was really nice to me, though it was obvious my lack of experience was a handicap so I did not ask to see her again.

Wendy had been a Grammar School girl and quite bright. Sam went to a secondary modern school and was nice. I had engaged my first tactile encounters with them, but I doubt, in retrospect, if I had done as much for their overall sexual experience as they had done for mine.

After Saturday nights at the cinema, for about two years, things started to happen with girls when a group of male friends and I began going to the local 'hop' in Boughrood Village Hall. A village hall is one of the focal points for community activity in rural areas – the others are pubs! The former are bleak in character. In those days they were usually made from wood, almost window less, and about the height of a two-storey house. Inside there is one very large room off which were several small annexes for tea making and cloakrooms. To say the least, they were inhospitable in appearance and similar in many ways to empty barns, the only difference being the wooden floors. The atmosphere they exuded was cold and lifeless, not at all conducive to the romance associated with soft lights and sweet music I saw on television and at the movies!

Before the dance my friends and I would visit the Griffin Inn in the neighbouring village of Llyswen. Here we would have several 'battery-charger' drinks to get us in the mood for talking to the girls and dancing that lay ahead.

Llyswen, Boughrood and Glasbury were neighbouring villages nestling in the foothills of the Black Mountains and the Begwns Hills on the borders of Breconshire and Radnorshire, now Powys. The River Wye ran lazily between them and gave the area much natural beauty. Geographically they lie between Builth Wells; home of the Royal Welsh Show in Wales, and the cathedral city of Hereford in England. Hay-on-Wye; the literary capital, is situated half way in-between, right on the Welsh - English border. By any standards the area is scenically very beautiful and much admired by the many thousands of visitors attracted here every year.

On such dance nights the last thing on my mind was 'natural' beauty except of the female variety. We danced to the worst pop music I could ever imagine. The local DJ was a farmer called Roy Herdman, and his music was suitably agricultural. By now I liked The Everly Brothers, Bill Haley, Buddy Holly, Del Shannon, Eddie Cochran and so forth; he played country and western! Everything was about 'lonesome cowboys' and had similarly catchy titles! The songs played every week were Kenny Price's *Oh Lonesome Me* and *Sea of Heartache* with *My Cheating Heart* by Hank Williams thrown in for good measure. Boy, did we rock the night away. The last two or three numbers every week were 'smooches'. If you had got lucky by now this was when you made your move. Needless to say I did not do much smooching!

Almost all the girls seemed to be farmer's daughters, although there were a few who were very much my kind, if only I could have got to grips with them! Several of them went to my school and from memory all of them were very nice and I actually got on rather well with most of them. My mother though put me off them immediately when she all too frequently insisted, "Jack you should *marry* a farmers' daughter. What about Dilys Hughes, now there's a lovely girl for you". Her reasoning was that they were always taught to be careful with money, had plenty of it, and would be the 'homely' type. I was terrified, the thought of it overwhelmed me – I would be found out!

By now whatever suggestion my mother made I rebelled against, so this idea was an absolute anathema to me. From my new discoveries into what made me, the alcoholic in the making 'tick', I now see that her 'controlling' ways all were blows to my ***pride***; yet another of my all too prominent defects of character. I did not like being told what to do by anyone at anytime *AND I always wanted my own way,* and when I did not get it I sulked. Today, I see this as another way of looking at ***greed and selfish, self-centredness,*** *yet more examples of the **seven deadly sins** I had in abundance* *featuring in my, as I saw it, rather pathetic little life.*

My parents owned a village shop. There were three other shops in the village and, as ours sold daily newspapers, it was easily the most frequented by customers. My parents worked 363 days a year, every year! In my eighteen years of living at home my father only once took a week's holiday. He had been a local lad with Shropshire blood, started work at age 14, and enjoyed a very simple country life - he had never been to London or abroad in his life and was not the slightest bit interested in either. His travel itinerary consisted of delivering local newspapers and groceries in a 3 mile radius, once a week visiting the local cash and carry in Hereford, visiting my mother's family once a month in Brecon and some years earlier the occasional visit to a football match in Birmingham or South Wales. To say the least he was not worldly, but I would say he was one of the most contented men I have ever met. All he needed to achieve this were his family, fishing, his garden, the pub and friends - and he had them all. So where I got my wanderlust from I do not know.

I admired my father very much then and even more now. Today I wish I had got to know him better before he died aged 68. He had been a real friend as well as a very kind and good man. Many were the Saturday afternoons he and I would sit 'glued' to the 'wireless' listening to his beloved Aston Villa, Cardiff City or Swansea Town football teams. At the time the latter two were First Division teams with revered footballers such as John Charles and Ivor Allchurch in their ranks. On other occasions we would spend hours listening to MCC versus Australia Test cricket matches with the likes of Bradman and Hutton scoring hundreds, whilst Lindwall, Miller, Truman and Laker took the wickets. As I write this nearly 50 years later I feel a yearning for those days to return; long before money and greed took over the sports, and some of the times I loved so much.

I liked sleeping in bed with my 'dad', it made me feel very safe. On one occasion, I remember going to his bedroom at about 3 o'clock in the morning to listen to Don Cockell fight Rocky Marciano for the world heavyweight boxing title at Madison Square Gardens in New York. Sadly the British hero got beaten badly by low punches that were allowed by the American referee. I recall having a big resentment against Marciano for this as well as serious ones some years later against Henry Cooper for flattening my Welsh hero, Joe Erskine. I was later to find out that **_resentment_** is considered the number one offender with regard to alcoholics' defects of character and that it 'kills' more of them than anything else! Little did I know I was already the perfect alcoholic in the making, as at this time I had not even had my first sip, except in sherry trifle and Christmas puddings rum sauce! (Both of which I adored.)

From around age 6 to 14, Blackpool, with Stanley Matthews and Stanley Mortenson as their stars, was my favourite football team. Their main competition came from Preston North End with Tom Finney, Newcastle United with Jacky Milburn and Bolton Wanderers with Nat Lofthouse. One of my best ever days was when they beat Bolton 3-2 in the 1953 FA Cup Final – I remember it well even though I was only 8 years old. We had just had television installed and we were one of the only homes in the village to have it. My friend Philip, a Bolton supporter, came around to watch. I had never been more passionate about a victory in my life. As soon as it was over he and I rushed into our garden to emulate our heroes. That day and most others at the time, I found it good to be alive. However I discovered the flip side of this later when losing almost anything was a horrendous experience and openly displayed my **_greed_** infested, **_self-centred_** mind.

As far as I can remember my father never once raised his voice to me or even told me off. Many times I can remember my mother criticising me for my laziness and unhelpfulness around our home, asking for his support and him always answering, "Leave the boy alone Kit, he's alright". I see today how he hated any form of confrontation whatsoever, but that this was not always the great quality of character I thought at the time. Then though, I was grateful as it meant I could carry on the way I liked. Retrospectively I see it would have been better if he had not always left my mother to apply all our household discipline, he should have shared some of the responsibility. Sadly, as the result, I ended up resenting my mother, which was grossly unfair as she was as good a mother as any I have witnessed. Fortunately she is still alive today aged 95 and in good health. As the result, for the past 22 years, I have been able to show her the love that I always felt but failed to deliver from age 15 to 40. After all, in no way was I a 'good' boy and some fatherly punishment may have addressed at least a few of my failings! In retrospect I have to say I had wonderful parents and my sister and I were blessed with much love and wise guidance over most of our formative years.

Even though there was much love in our household the actual word 'love' was never used between my parents and me. Years later I found this was something I had in common with many others of a similar age brought up in the western world. I find this sad today and assume it was some sort of throwback to Victorian attitudes. It is my view that this attitude, and that of not 'talking' about sex, are part of the foundations that have caused many of the marital problems that prevail today. It certainly did with me as I grew up being ashamed to even watch kissing in front of my mother and father on television. Even today aged 62 I notice I still feel a little uncomfortable, though it is infinitely better than it used to be. When I look back at my mental mayhem surrounding love and sex I realise how serious my psychological problems were and fully understand why I was later to need external stimulants to provide me with confidence when dealing with life and girls.

Then there was my first wet dream! I had not a clue what had happened. I woke up with this warm, sticky stuff on my hand and me wondering what on earth it was. I was 16 and no one had educated me as to how babies were conceived. I had heard the 'big' boys talking but I was always too ashamed to admit my ignorance. I used to pretend I knew, just like many other things that I did not know about in life. I thought that if they knew what I was really like they would not want to know me. This form of ***dishonesty*** I now see was part of my ***pride,*** as under no circumstances did I want to be 'found out' and for everyone to think me stupid. When I added these to my well-established habits of lying and stealing, (easier to understand forms of ***dishonesty***), I realised all I had done was to hammer further huge nails into my coffin of ***self- loathing*** and ***self pity.***

I was to become a child of the so-called promiscuous society of 'free love' in the 1960's and 70's. But for me this was a tag that I could never accept about myself, my moral attitudes were so well embedded. If I could have 'accepted' it I would probably not have come to so deeply detest the very promiscuous person I became years later. Today it would seem this 'free love' had its foundations as a society's rebellion towards the unnatural rigidity of the Victorian moral attitudes to sex that were still rife in my parents generation and passed on to me. This was typified when girls in my village became pregnant outside wedlock and were immediately classified as outcasts. Similarly, when one of my friends started dating a black girl from Hay-on-Wye, his parents banned him from seeing her. I also saw this same attitude applied to the village 'drunks', a graphic picture I was to remember with horror as my own alcoholism set in: ***"I am an outcast, an unwanted member of society - a leper"*** I realised.

Today, I blame much of the chaos and confusion surrounding broken homes, including the breakdown of my own marriage, on the unnaturalness surrounding the sex climate that still exists. As the result, my generation took sex from one extreme to another, we spanned the gap of reasonableness without a bridge in between. Ask any child who has a single parent which would they consider best from a healthy home point of view, one parent or two? The answer 99 times out of 100 will be two, which will be based on their experience and what they have witnessed with envy in two parent families. Today in the West, we still have a legacy where sex is a 'big thing', very much in the open yet still causing chaos. Until this is removed, mayhem in boy/girl relationships will continue to reign.

It is my great hope and belief that in the next several generations a balanced attitude will eventually be found: one which sits naturally with us as human beings, not one that is manipulated by the media or by past ridiculously rigid, or Hollywood style, love story, attitudes. I am convinced that a levelling out will one day come into being due to a wiser approach. It will then replace a way of life that is clearly bad, causes instability and does not work versus one that is good and would work. One possible way to get to this point may be to put the experience of the world's people and its customs regarding sex and marriage into one big, fact based 'melting pot', and the results permeated by computer to find the way forward, which would work best.

At weekends I became a paperboy. Saturdays I especially hated. All my mates were allowed a lie-in. There was no school and I was the only one who had to get up and work. Boy did I feel sorry for myself and chronic **_self-pity_** became another devastating shortcoming of mine. Every Saturday morning I set off on my bicycle, whistling *The Dam Busters March* for about two hours of what I thought was sheer hardship. The whistling was to try to put on a brave face and to attempt to cheer myself up, 'Whistle a happy tune' from 'The King and I' was a big hit at the time. Never did I think of helping my parents as giving something back to them; it was just **_selfish_** me, me, me, all the time!

Sundays were almost as bad, but at least we delivered the

23

papers in our car that day and we started an hour later. I always liked being with my father and this was a great opportunity to spend time with him, time to enjoy listening to his views on sport and life. Also, there was a girl's residential school we used to deliver to that day *and* Diana's farm, another of my favourite delivery points, was en route as well!

The only time I enjoyed delivering the papers was at Christmas as many of my customers gave me a tip – usually 2s 6d - about £3.00 in present-day money I suspect. It was also then that I was introduced to the warm winter wonders of alcohol. It was very cold in this part of Wales this time of year and I was frequently given a glass of sherry, Drambuie or ginger wine to keep out the frost; at last I had found heaven! I was also given lots of yummy liqueur chocolates. I had the 'gift of the gab', was quite a sweet looking child, and many of my customers were older ladies whom I found it easy to 'butter' up. By fifteen I was coming home 'tipsy' regularly and loved it.

Our house was detached and had once been a flourishing farmhouse. It had meat hooks, a scullery, beams and a large attic that gave it the type of character much sought-after today. There were numerous outbuildings, pigsties, cow sheds, barns and so forth. All in all it was a great home to grow up in. There was a big garden, big enough for playing football and cricket; also a wall where I learned to hit tennis balls. Our garden backed onto a wood, which was a wonderful outlet for my play as I grew up. Here I would go birds nesting and learned much about nature in a truly natural way: though I was not aware of how much I had learned and how much I loved it until I found sobriety some 30 years later.

On the other three sides of our house things were vastly different. In four of the eight houses surrounding us lived someone of unsound mind; each had spent time in a mental institution! In fact on one occasion the lady from the house immediately across the road had come into our shop and attacked my father or mother (I cannot remember which) with a huge carving knife! She claimed my father had been serenading her under her bedroom window the night before! She was locked up for a long time as the result. It had been a scary few minutes and my mother had rushed me into a room in the middle of the house for protection. I was aged 8 and was petrified; the paralysis of **_fear_** of personal injury was by now my constant companion.

It was that kind of village all right: much beauty and madness all around. Our shop sold sweets amongst many other things. From an early age I can remember pilfering from it regularly. As I grew up I did the same in other shops whenever I thought I could get away with it. The only time I was caught by my mother was when I had stolen a Cadburys Cream Egg and put it in my shirt breast pocket. When asked by her what the bulge was under my sweater I said, "It's nothing!" She felt it, and for the first time I was caught red-handed. She scolded me severely for **_lying and stealing,_** but it did not stop me; I just became more careful! I was about nine at the time.

Every day our school bus would stop at the local tuck shop on our way home from school. On each visit another boy, known as 'Strawberry' because it rhymed with his name, and I had a competition to see who could steal the most sweets, chocolates and crisps – this became my standard behaviour for several years, though on these occasions I never got caught. Looking back, I wondered what difference it would have made if I had?

There was another instance when I was caught stealing. I was about ten years old, and my mother and I had gone to stay with some family friends called Thomas. They were very kind and we were having an extremely enjoyable holiday in Kidderminster in the Midlands. They had four sons and one of them had a fine collection of stamps. I only had a few so literally stole almost all of his. When the theft was discovered I automatically denied it but the game was up when they were found in my possession. Needless to say, this caused huge embarrassment for all concerned, especially my mother and me! Reflecting on these incidents today it would appear I was none too bright as well!

As well as my more blatant **_dishonesty_** with regard to lying and stealing, I went to extraordinary lengths to cover up my true personality. In my early teens, Adam Faith and Cliff Richard vied for the number one British, male, pop singer slot. I liked "Cliff" more, but I claimed to like "Adam" as "Cliff" was regarded as sissyish. This was a pattern I was to portray throughout my addictive years and in many areas. Analysing it in retrospect I realise how adopting this behaviour was **_dishonest,_** I did it to stop my **_pride_** being dented and was riddled with my usual **_self- centredness_**. The bottom line again being that I did not want anyone to know what I was really like, so I would lie about almost anything.

I also suffered from 'the grass is always greener on the other side' syndrome! This is much unheralded as a serious problem, but ask any alcoholic or drug addict and they will tell you they have it in abundance. In my case it was always based on **_envy_** and caused me much **_self-pity, and_** when bad enough, could cause me serious mental depression. As the result I was put on anti-depressants several times. The trouble with anti-depressants is that they take three days to start working while addicts like me only want 'quick fixes': so another defect, **_impatience_** reared its ugly head.

The trouble was I took **_envy_** to new extremes. *I had envied EVERY single person I had ever met! I made a list of all those I had past resentments towards and I found EVERYONE had something or someone in their lives I wished I had.* This was a hell of a mouthful for me swallow at the time and even today I find it hard to believe; yet it was a fact. They were either richer, lived in a bigger home, had a more prestigious car, better looking, more intelligent, had nicer parents, better at sport, less cowardly, happily married, had a better job, or had a nicer girlfriend than I had. And so it went on, the list was ad infinitum. So everything in my life seemed negative and I had depressions!

This major flaw in my make-up became most apparent to me one Christmas. I had been given a second-hand Raleigh bicycle by my parents as my 'number one' present. Christmas day afternoon I met up with my friends. All three had *"new Hercules"*. That was all it took to saddle me with huge envy! I did not like that bike from that moment on. I did not once think of the kindness of my parents and the trouble they had gone to to get it and as the result I took my _**self- pity**_ to new dimensions.

My father used to say about my self-centredness, "Self first, self last, any over self again." Boy was he right, though I did not know to what extent at the time.

From an early age I had a built-in love of wildlife, especially insects and birds. Yet I stole birds' eggs, pulled off the legs and wings of insects and, worst of all for me, shot at little birds with an air rifle. To this day I do not understand how I could do this given my hatred of physical pain inflicted on any living creature? It certainly did not help me to love the person I really was, but at that time I did not know that this was a fundamental rule in learning to love oneself.

To add to my further misery I bullied boys younger or physically weaker than myself. Today I abhor bullying of any sort, at any level, seeing it as a most horrible and cowardly act. I now believe I bullied because of my chronically low _**self-esteem,**_ which is no excuse, but knowing the reason has helped my current better understanding of the nature of me as an adolescent. This understanding was essential for my future growth as I was later able to forgive myself for this, along with everything else I hated about me and my past. For my first forty years it had seemed that from every direction I looked at myself I saw an almost evil 'monster' looking back at me, an image I absolutely despised.

There were several aspects about owning the village shop I thoroughly enjoyed. One was serving certain older, female customers. I found by teasing them and using my innocent looks and youth, I could get away with lots. Whenever 'Mrs Miles' or 'Miss Morgan' came into our shop my mood lifted immediately; it was as if there was a trigger of mischievousness set off in me. I would instantly become witty, almost cheeky, but not quite! It taught me much about the narrow tightrope I would later walk, about what I could or could not say and get away with - all good experience for the amateur conman I was later to become.

This sharp-witted attribute I was soon able to put to good use and did so frequently! Aged 16 I was caught cheating in a GCE 'O' level exam. I was hauled before the headmaster, Mr Howells, a very nice man. I was terrified as he got out his cane and told me to bend down. I braced myself as I bent over but immediately I started talking, telling him some incredible 'cock-and-bull' story to try to get out of it. I could not believe it when he said, "Okay, I will let you off this time, but make sure nothing like it ever happens again!" (It was not too many years later that caning was banned as a school punishment, but in my day it was still a formidable threat, which I for one was always afraid of).

For a number of years after this I was 'cocky' and believed I could get away with almost, anything. What I did not realise was that I was *never* getting away with anything in the long run.

As a youth I loved gambling. I started playing brag and poker when I was about 14. I was not particularly gifted as a player but I did love taking risks. By the time I was 15 I had organised a gambling syndicate at my school every day and at my home every night. I had influenced older boys from the upper and lower sixth to play with me; boys mostly aged

17 and 18. At school we played mostly in the toilets for fear of being caught. Needless to say we were caught, and as I was the known ringleader, I faced another hiding from the head master. I think he must have liked me as again he listened to my excuses and let me off without serious punishment. I had begun to realise I was good at this 'chat' stuff *and* of course it was a great story to tell my mates! ***Anything that impressed I saw as an improvement on the real me.***

At the time I developed my terrible inferiority complex with regard to sex, I had become infatuated with boy/girl "love" stories. From the magazines in my parents' shop, every day at about aged 15, I would come home from school and bury myself in silly romantic comics. They all portrayed this kind of love as idyllic, "happy ever after," affairs. They were aimed at the teenage girl market and ***definitely*** not for boys. This was the late 1950's and they contained no sex whatsoever, only kissing, which was usually on the very last page! These ridiculous stories became my role models for life and I now see how horribly back to front I had got it.

Each girl and boy in every story behaved almost perfectly and I carried this attitude towards girls with me for many years to come. I actually used to think the very pretty ones were near perfect for that was exactly how they were portrayed in the comics! Often I would put them on 'pedestals' and refused to believe it when I was told, "such and such", whom I adored, was not a virgin. In other words I lived in a world of sheer fantasy too. Even today some of this attitude still haunts me but being aware of it has meant I have adjusted to the real world and grown up just a little. I still have the view "sleeping around" is not right, but now at least I can accept my past behaviour as having been that of a sick person, one who was extraordinarily ***lonely*** and desperately sought comfort through drugs and sex. So ***Lust,*** coupled with my ***self-centered loneliness***, I now saw were more of my many defects of character that had to be straightened out if ever I was going to recover from chronic addiction.

Needless to say, as I came to realise more deeply my imperfections regarding sex, I learned to loathe myself even more. The guilt of my own promiscuity seriously damaged any last threads of decency I had regarding my already shredded self-esteem. At this point, *I knew I was bad in regard to every aspect of my life* and there was nowhere to hide, accept in alcohol and drugs.

Chapter 2

A LIFE OF GRIME.

Although my many character defects did not lead me to a life of more serious crime, I see today how easily they could have. What they did do was form the pattern of how I would live my life for the next twenty-five years – teetering on the edge, looking over my shoulder for *fear* of being caught in whatever wrongdoing I was committing.

The extraordinary thing was that in 1963, aged 18, I joined the police force! This was always a mistake and with hindsight would seem to have been one of the biggest I ever made. I simply did not fit in. I was a coward, rebel, liar and thief; conditions totally unsuited to police work. Within 2½ years I was hated by almost every policeman I worked with, due mostly to my rebellious attitude towards authority and acute laziness.

I had to start as a police cadet because of my age. The only requirements for joining were a reasonable intelligence, good eyesight and to be over 5 foot 9 inches tall! Pay was okay and I thought the uniform would attract the girls. I was stationed at Herefordshire's police headquarters and put to work in the criminal intelligence department (CID). I was really just a filing clerk. I worked under a nice Welshman who was a Detective Constable, a kindly Detective Sergeant and a very gentlemanly Detective Chief Inspector. Also there was a secretary and another cadet. I was quite content and found reading the criminal records on the file cards quite interesting.

Aged 19 I qualified to become a police constable. I was sent to the police training centre in Bridgend, Glamorganshire. Here I made some good friends and at least some of the time I was quite enjoying myself. I guess it was a lot like being in the army. We slept in bunks in a room of about 14 of us, were up at the crack of dawn and did a lot of marching. There were lots of dress inspections and much classroom work. We were being taught the basic rudiments of criminal and civil law. I should have excelled here but again I did little work and stayed near the bottom of my class.

Then came the big day, I was to be 'sworn in'. For my 19th birthday my parents had bought me a gleaming, jet black Austin A30 car of which I was truly proud. On the following Saturday morning I was released from classes in Bridgend to drive to Hereford for the ceremony. I set off in good time and had just crossed the stunningly beautiful Brecon Beacon mountain range. It was icy and a little foggy. I was on a fairly straight road, when coming around a bend some 100 yards or so in front of me, was a Land Rover. I panicked, hit the brakes to hard, and within 3 seconds my world had literally turned upside down! I will never forget the sensation or what went through my mind. I kept asking myself as the car rolled over, "At what moment will I die?" I did not even get a scratch and it soon slid to a stop having turned one half somersault and landed on its side in a ditch. I got out and surveyed the scene. I felt pathetic and completely stupid.

After gathering my thoughts I walked a few hundred yards and found a telephone kiosk. I telephoned home and told my mother 'a version' of what had happened. Fortunately she was just relieved I that I was okay. Eventually it was arranged that the D.C.I. would collect me, which he duly did. He was very kind about my accident but for the whole of my journey I felt to embarrassed to even talk. The **_self-obsessed_**, full of **_pride_** 'me' took over and for once I found a humility I did not know I even had.

After police training I was stationed at Ross-on-Wye, a small town in Herefordshire. It was called "sleepy" by the locals because hardly anything ever happened there. My being there though seemed to change all that!

One Sunday night I went on duty at 10.00pm with my partner, Wally. There was a lot of noise coming from near the town centre. He told me to go one way and he would go the other, catching the perpetrators somewhere in the middle. Being no hero I took my time! When I reached him he was talking to three young men and telling one of them in particular to behave himself. Suddenly he drew back his fist and hit him hard in the stomach. I was as stunned as the youth who did not seem to have done anything. He added a few words of wisdom to the doubled up lad about his future behaviour and off we went. A few yards down the road Wally explained his actions, "The lad's just come out of borstal and that'll teach him to behave".

Next day the youth's mother made a complaint about the 'assault'. An internal investigation was carried out and I was interviewed. I refused to say that the policeman had been provoked which was what he claimed. I wish I could now say this was due to my honesty and desire to see justice done, but it was all due to my rebellious nature. I was, "Sent to Coventry" by most of my colleagues and that was how it remained for the rest of my time as a policeman.

A sitting was arranged for a few weeks later to hear the case the mother was bringing against her son's attacker. Now I am not suggesting for one moment that the police manipulated what happened next but these are the facts. On the weekend before the case was to be heard the following happened: we had a 'Dad's Army' type of Inspector at our police station; getting on in years, about to retire and had been in Ross for as long as anyone could remember. The local townsfolk adored him. On the Saturday night before the hearing was due he just happened to be in a local pub and was 'attacked' by the same youth! The youth was charged with assaulting a police officer and locked up until Monday morning. His hearing was arranged to take place *immediately before* his against Wally. Needless to say he was found guilty as charged and Wally got off. I was only asked in my evidence if I had seen the policeman provoked and of course I had not. Case dismissed, as it was deemed the youth may have made a 'sudden movement' which only Wally had seen, one which meant he may have been going for a knife in his pocket and was about to stab Wally to death with me and the other two looking on.

There were other interesting experiences I had in the police force. My police shifts ran from 6am to 2pm, 2pm to 10pm and 10pm to 6am. I loathed "nights" as I was convinced there were dangers lurking behind every corner. 'Ross' though was not called "sleepy" for nothing! The most serious crime I ever dealt with was the theft of a pedal cycle: maximum sentence life imprisonment or death by hanging! So I really had very little to worry about, but worry I did and **_fear_** haunted my every move after midnight.

Night duties usually started well. After signing on at 10pm, Wally and I would go to a local hostelry where the owner would ply us with free drinks after closing time at 10.30pm. There was a 10 minute drinking up time, and once all the regulars had left, we took over! Pubs needed licenses and we, the police, controlled them! Landlords buttered us up in the only way they knew how and several drinks later I had enough courage to face the night ahead. Often I had several drinks before going on duty as well, so the first hour or two would pass quite comfortably.

Most nights followed this pattern though there was sometimes the odd exception and it was always in the "wee, small hours" that I would be caught unawares. Once when pushing my bicycle up the hill alongside the town church, a cat jumped off a wall onto my shoulder and quickly off again, frightening me almost to death. But this was nothing to what happened a few weeks later! I was methodically checking to see that the town's shop doors were locked, a duty we carried out every night. Almost never was one left open, so by 3am I would become quite lackadaisical in my attitude, as I would have checked a dozen or more streets by that time. I then took almost for granted the rest of the town was locked up safely too!

One particular night I had just checked the High Street bank and as casually as ever, put my hand on the jewellers door handle next door. To my shock and horror it opened! Standing less than two yards in front of me was a man staring straight back at me. I had my police helmet on and I swear my hair 'literally' stood on end! I could not believe it. For that instant I was paralysed.

My next revelation was that I was looking at me! The outer door had opened inwards and a security door with a full-length mirror facing the street was directly inside. I was looking at a full length reflection of myself! I have never felt more stupid in all my life. I ran to tell my partner, not about my terror, but about the open door. As I reached him I realised I had not checked the inner door but decided to hell with that, as there might be burglars on the other side! I did not think for one second that with me running away they might escape! Wally admonished me, for he was no hero either and knew that as the senior officer he had the checking I had left undone still to do. Of course these were no burglars, the jeweller was called and life in "sleepy" Ross got back to normal. Wally never told anyone about my _**fear**_ driven shortcomings and for that I was eternally grateful, especially in light of my failure to support him in his hour of need a few months earlier!

At around this time the most extraordinary event of all took place in my short police career. It was Sunday afternoon on as sultry a day as Ross had ever known, just like any other Sunday at 1.45pm in this sort of English market town. Most homes would be half way through their Sunday roast and the families about to relax for the rest of the day. I had just wheeled my bicycle into the road and was casually looking left and right. I stopped almost mortified! Ross was about to go into the British crime history books forever and I was to be its star witness. My legendary cowardice turned horizontal as I put my foot on a pedal and surveyed the scene where two hundred yards to my left along the busy A40, cars were ramming each other head on. I could not believe my eyes and high tailed it to the right in the opposite direction. Fortunately that was the way to the police station too. As I arrived there, the duty officer was just receiving a call reporting the "incident". I stayed "mum" knowing that if I told anyone what I had witnessed at first hand, and my reaction to it, I would have been in terrible trouble; labelled the biggest coward ever to don a uniform and probably booted out unceremoniously.

It turned out that the night before, lads from the Forest of Dean had come into Ross and had got into a punch-up with some local Ross hard men. The police had put a stop to it and arrested several of the culprits. Their mates had decided to return the next day and 'sort things out'. I knew nothing about this and thanked God for that, otherwise I may not have turned up for duty that day, and by now I was wishing I had not.

The car ramming situation was resolved by my fellow officers and a few more arrests were made. By now all the local policemen and squad cars in the county had been summoned to the Ross-on- Wye police station. I kept a very low profile. Word had it that the local hard men and the "Foresters" as they were called, had now teamed up and were on their way to 'attack' the police station and free their friends. "Oh my God", I thought, "what the hell am I going to do?" I had never been more afraid in my life.

By 5 o'clock everyone was very tense. It was obvious no one had a clue what to do; how could they? No one had ever experienced anything like it before. Suggestions were made and orders given. We were to wait for our Inspector's instructions. Fortunately there was a sergeant who was as cool as a cucumber. He was ex-SAS and one of the hardest men I ever met. It was as if his body and mind were made of granite, he even wore his police boots without socks! That afternoon I followed him like a lamb wherever he went. I think he saw right through me to my yellow belly but never once did he let on or treat me other than with absolute kindness.

At 6 o'clock we heard "they" were on the march and heading

for the back entrance to the police station. In front of the rear entrance was a large, open car park – an ideal spot for "them" to launch "their" attack. The trouble was they had not accounted for the one little old 'Dad's Army' Inspector in our pack who had other ideas! He ordered all his 'troops' to assemble outside the back door to the station.

There were by now about 25 of us and he told us to stand three deep on the station steps. I stood at the back in the middle wondering what on earth was going to happen next. After about 10 minutes our lookout came running back, "They're by the fire station and will be here in two or three minutes". There were a few mumbles otherwise no one said a thing.

There were probably 25 of them or so too. As they came around the corner into the car park my already 1,000 strong butterfly stomach turned cartwheels. No one had ever told me life as a policeman could be as bad as this. Thirty meters away from us they started to slow down. Our Inspector gave the first order. "Attent.....ion!" We did as we were told. The marchers slowed down even more. Next the Inspector ordered, "Draw truncheons". We did. Then he said the immortal word, "C-H-A-R-G-E".

I had never seen or done anything like it in my life; twenty or so policemen running full tilt at the oncoming "mob". It must have been a sight to behold. I actually joined in though I stayed near the back out of harm's way. One of my colleagues, rugby tackled one of the slower "baddies" who was putting up very little fight and I dived on top of them both. Within minutes, several were arrested and the rest disappeared.

Back in the police station there was total confusion. "What could "they" be charged with was everyone's question?" No one had a clue. CID were asked but they did not know either. Then someone mentioned, "an affray". What was that most of us wondered? And "an affray" it became whether it was or not. From memory there had only ever been one or two recorded affrays by the whole British police force before that fateful Sunday! So 'sleepy' little Ross-on-Wye made the history books of British crime and my secret, "eye witness" account has lived with me to this day.

By this time, my normal way of rebelling was not to 'book' anyone. After six months of my taking this attitude I was hauled before the station superintendent and asked to explain my conduct. I made some feeble excuses but inwardly fought every word. I was then ordered to 'book' a particular streets' parking offenders. As I walked there, I noticed our 'Dad's Army' Inspector's wife's car illegally parked! I triumphantly wrote out a ticket and displayed it on her windscreen. I deliberately did not 'book' anyone else. I was deliriously happy but knew I was headed for trouble. The outcome was inevitable and I resigned before they had time to fire me.

Around this period my Saturday nights were spent at the local dancehall in Wormelow Hall, a huge mansion on the outskirts of Hereford. I mostly went with Sue to see groups such as the "The Searchers", "The Swinging Blue Jeans", "Gerry and the Pacemakers", "Brian Poole and the Tremeloes" and so forth. They were the backbone of the "Merseybeat", the sound of Liverpool. The Beatles were the 'front bone' but they never quite made it to Hereford!

Sue was attractive and had a great figure but, as I said earlier, was a not too bright hairdresser. She lived at home and after the dance we had, for me, the highlight of the evening was a long "snog" on the front seat of my car. This was an Austin Metropolitan: a poor man's replica of a sports car, but it was the best I could afford given my policeman's salary and actually, I was really very proud of it. It was a 2 seater, two tone in colour and quite rare. They had been especially made for the American servicemen in Europe I was told, so almost 'American' and therefore cool I thought! My idea was to impress the girls. Unfortunately for me it was mostly the lead singer of "The Searchers" that did that for Sue! However, I doted on her and when she finished our relationship I was wrecked. I had gone home to stay with my parents the night it happened and my mother's answer was a large brandy. I quickly discovered that *several of these worked wonders and fixed* **all** *problems*! **One tasted good but several really did the trick.**

I had worked in an office in Hereford briefly before joining the police force. There I met Avril and at this time we started dating. Avril was more 'experienced' than Sue and helped put back together my 'broken heart'. Suddenly one night I realised I could hide why I was a virgin no longer as Avril and I were heading for serious sex! I ran, or more appropriately squirmed, a mile! I had the car started and headed back towards Ross as quick as a 'bat out of hell'; that was where the _*fear*_ of revealing my 'unmanliness' immediately took me.

This brief encounter though, brought Sue running back to me, but this time my ego took over and dictated the direction our dalliance was to go. *This time I was 'in charge', a role I liked but one which caused me huge problems later as in most situations in my life I discovered I was not 'in charge'. In other words I discovered that I was totally*

'POWERLESS' over much of what takes place even in my life. Today I see how this was more of the same _self-centredness_ and _greed_ I now noted from my earlier life. The trouble was from now on I was also alone with no one to turn to for help *and* I had too much _pride_ to ask anyone for advice. So for now with Sue I decided where we went, how often we met and what we did. However, I soon lost interest in this as I always did when I kept getting my own way and moved on.

But now I had discovered I loved "a challenge". What I could not have I would put up one hell of a fight for and when I had what I wanted I usually lost interest. The real trouble was that most of the time I did not get what I wanted and that's when much of my extremes of _self-pity_ kicked in – I had never been told that I was _powerless_ over much of what happened in life. These occasions, almost always made threadbare my emotions and ended in tears, with massive doses of prolonged mental torture (i.e. depression) thrown in for good measure! On each occasion now though I had alcohol to pull me through, I had discovered a magic 'pick-me-up' potion! Little did I know that years later I would discover that I had been totally _powerless_ over the effects of alcohol too. Much to my surprise, the great 'me' was to discover 20 years on, that this was a condition I had in common with every other alcoholic and drug addict on our planet.

Ironically in recovery, I was to find the condition of _'POWERLESSNESS'_ was to play a positive role in my life when I eventually found recovery and that there was a positive angle to this I would not in a million years have thought of by myself!.

We were now well into the "swinging sixties". I loved the Beatles and most of the other groups around at the time. My dates up until then had all been with working class girls who were a lot like me – their likes and dislikes I had grown up with. This all changed dramatically!

Whilst in my digs as a policeman, I befriended a middle-class vet who lived there too. He was suave, cool, good-looking and ex-public school – I envied him hugely. Mostly, though, he was a great success with middle-class girls! He called himself 'Slim' and because of his terrific looks and physique could get away with it! For the next five years I learned to copy him in almost everything. I changed the way I spoke, dressed, whom I associated with, where I ate etc. I even found a girlfriend who looked like his. I started to work on dropping my Welsh accent and many of my working-class friends. *I had come to want more than anything else to change EVERYTHING about me. The only question was could I do it?*

At this time, 1965, I joined Cadbury Brothers plc as a sales representative. Here I quickly learned the art of fiddling an expense account. My main job was as a 'relief' representative. I would be sent all over the United Kingdom standing in for reps that were sick or on holiday.

One of my main secondments was to Northern Ireland. I worked in all the counties and learned to love the country and the people. On reflection it was also very interesting, as the 'troubles' only started a few years later.

I first arrived one Monday morning at about 8.30 a.m. I had flown to Belfast from Birmingham on an early, direct flight. My taxi took me straight into the city centre. I could not believe my eyes when suddenly, passing a bus stop, I saw two men fighting hammer and tongs. Remember, this was in 1965, *before* the troubles started! I soon discovered there was segregation in Northern Ireland, which was almost as bad as apartheid in South Africa. Catholics were just not allowed to go to Protestant schools. Some pavements in the Shankhill Road area were painted red, white and blue. Belfast was a bubble waiting to burst, and sure enough it did with much bloodshed shortly after.

In the next thirteen years I had similar jobs with Colgate-Palmolive and Xerox Corporation. My expense-fiddling behaviour did not change, but my lifestyle certainly did!

Chapter 3

THE LURE OF CITY LIGHTS

It was now 1968. I had moved to London, where I got a job selling toiletries and household cleaning products with Colgate Palmolive. There, I quickly learned how to manipulate sales target returns as well as cheat expenses. My figures so impressed the sales director that I became his blue-eyed boy. As a result I was promoted for each of the next three years. With each promotion I was given more money and greater flexibility with my expense account. In my last position as National Accounts Manager, I was allowed 'open' airline and train tickets. This meant that all I had to do was fill in the information as to my journey and they were ready for use. I could not believe my luck. And so it went on with my making and fiddling more money than I had ever dreamed of, whilst climbing ever higher up the social ladder.

At this time, through my girlfriend Jen's brother Michael, I was introduced to the world of Carnaby Street style men's fashion and London's much revered, swinging night-life. Michael was in the rag trade, owned his own boutiques and drove an MGB BT convertible – the *only* car to be seen in at the time: Triumphs and Sunbeams were second best to the Chelsea set!

Every Thursday night we went to the De Vere Club on Kensington High Street. His friends there were; Brad, a buyer for Ballantyne's Cashmere House; 'Dave', a top male model, and two other men in the same business. The King's Road style, mini-skirt clad, long-legged, super-slim Mary

Quant type 'chicks' who hung out there loved being with these well-groomed 'trendies' – and for social climbing reasons so did I! The trouble was, none of the 'chicks' were the slightest bit interested in a household cleaning products and toothpaste salesman! More bad news for my lowly *self-esteem*! The blokes liked me though, because of my friendship with Michael and, I guess, the lack of competition I provided - which for now was all that really mattered to me. Looking back I can see I just did not 'fit in' but that did not stop my desires for upward mobility taking over.

Their glamorous world became a completely new way of life for me. From now on it was 'down the King's Road' with Michael on Saturday afternoons, Chelsea discos and South Ken parties at night.

At one of these parties I met Gay and meeting her was to change my life forever. I had lived in the 'grass is always greener on the other side' syndrome for years and here was the chance to change my life forever. She had the looks, style, grace, intelligence and status I was seeking. Her father was 'in the City' and chairman of a well-known establishment institution

Gay lived in Knightsbridge near *The Australian* pub. In typical London style she shared a house with three other girls, Barbara, Elizabeth and Greta. They were all ex public school and had prestigious City jobs. They each had a great social life with cocktail parties, boyfriends, lunches, dinners and the theatre as their regular weekly diet. I had never been to a cocktail party in my life but quickly discovered they were all about drinking and meeting people of the opposite sex – I soon found myself completely at home!

For most midweek dates I went to Gay's place for early

evening cocktails. I loved this, as I was usually the first male to arrive and often had the four girls all to myself. Over and over I sat with them talking about the latest events in their ever-so-full lives, whilst the music from 'Un Homme et Une Femme', Simon and Garfunkel's 'Bridge Over Troubled Water' and Carole King's 'Tapestry' played in the background. I now believed I was the luckiest man in the world and that life had not been, and could never get, better than this. I had at last found love and a way of life beyond my wildest dreams. At least, that was what I thought!

Most Sundays I went to Gay's Northwood family home for lunch. Here I was introduced to 'Gin and French' and 'Gin and It' - 'Dad pours large ones only,' she had said. I liked him straight away! With our meals we drank fine wines such as Pouilly Fuisse and Nuits St Georges. On special occasions we drank champagne. I made a point of remembering the names of these and they quickly became my 'favorite drinks'! We also had 'starters' for lunch - not 'dinner', as I had been brought up to call it. These included avocado pears, artichokes, prawns, caviar, truffles, smoked salmon and other wonders of my strange 'new world'. At that time such foods were classified as luxuries and not the everyday foods several of them are today. *And* I had to learn how to eat them. This was not always easy, especially the artichokes and unshelled prawns which, when they were put on my plate for the first time, baffled me completely. I quickly learned to watch others eat first, not daring to show my ignorance by asking how they should be eaten!

I was also learning a new language! I discovered 'canapés', the difference between napkins and serviettes, as well as how to pronounce Beauchamp Place in Knightsbridge! Not 'Beau Champs' as I had always called it but 'Beecham!'

But it was not only new words Gay introduced me too!

I was 25 and still a virgin. Most Sundays when we did not go to her parents we went to 'The Australian' for pre-lunch drinks. On one of these occasions we went back to her place to eat. I opened a bottle of wine and then another. Her housemates were all away. We were listening to Claude Lelouche's famous soundtrack and got into heavy petting. We went to the bedroom where we undressed and lay naked next to one other for the first time.

The alcohol had given me confidence and I tried to say, 'Would you like to have sex?' Instead I said, 'I know you are a virgin like me, and your mum and dad would not like it, but would it be okay if we try to have a *little* sex?' The words stumbled out and must have sounded extraordinarily unromantic and quite pathetic.

She lay there in deep bliss, looking longingly wonderful and I knew it was all right to continue. I do not believe she heard a word I said.

In seconds it was all finished. I rolled over and onto my back and lit a cigarette just like I had seen in the movies. For several minutes I lay there wondering, 'Why is there so much fuss talked about sex?' But I did not say a word as I gradually realized that it was meant to have lasted much longer!

Immediately my ego took another almighty splattering. I did not dare ask her how it had been for her as I was convinced she was loathing me and that this view was going to last forever. Now I knew for certain I was the least manly man ever to have existed; not that I needed much convincing! Though in fact, our affair continued for almost another year.

Meeting Gay also introduced me to the 'grass-is-always-greener-on-the-other-side' syndrome with regard to *all* girls - I already had it in abundance regarding everything else from years of *envy* when comparing myself - and my possessions - with everyone with whom I had grown up. Now I was to suffer with it even more as my years of searching for Miss Perfect in the world of romantic love were about to start in earnest!

Gay was the girl I was sure I adored above every other girl in the world, and Miss Perfect for me. On my first visit to have lunch with her parents, I had driven to Northwood on a bright Sunday morning with not a care in the world. I was to meet the mother and father of the girl I knew I would marry and with whom I would live happily ever after. Little did I know what lay in store only minutes after I parked the car!

Gay had told me that her father was a stickler for punctuality. Terrified of getting it wrong, I arrived precisely at 1 o'clock for pre-lunch drinks. As I surveyed their large house and gardens from the driveway my confidence took a huge jolt and my stomach fluttered with a thousand butterflies. I had never been to a grander house than this since the days I had played cricket with Johnny Royds, one of the Wedgewoods, when I was 10 and 11 years old in Glasbury-on-Wye.

'THIS is where my girl lives?' I kept saying to myself.

I rang the doorbell. Moments later I heard footsteps coming to the door, and a dog barking. The door opened and there to my astonishment was as stunningly beautiful a young lady as I had ever set eyes upon. I could not believe what I was seeing. I just peered at the gorgeous, radiant face that was smiling back at me and froze.

'*WHO the hell is this*?' I was screaming to myself.

She continued to smile mischievously as only a girl who knows what she's got can, and said, 'You must be Jack. I'm Beatrice, Gay's sister. Most people call me Trixie,' throwing her fair hair back from her lovely face as she did so.

I just stood there speechlessly swooning. Gay no longer stood a chance; my eyes feasted on this youthful, sparkling visage as she continued to smile and said, 'Gay will be down in a minute. I'm doing some painting upstairs. Would you like to come and see or would you prefer a drink in the bar whilst you wait' I did not need a second invitation to either; but the drink took precedence as it always did!

By now her equally attractive mother had appeared in the hallway and immediately made me feel at ease; she always had that way about her. I suspected she guessed what was going through my mind and that the awful guilt-ridden desire for her youngest daughter that I was suddenly feeling was etched all over my being.

Several minutes later Gay came downstairs. As always she exuded happiness and looked terrific, but in that instant her presence no longer did for me what it had always done before. To say the least, I was confused by this extraordinary turn of events and thanked God that her mother quickly gave me another very large drink.

As if realizing what had happened Gay said: 'I see you have

met *my little sister.'*

I sheepishly grinned and replied, 'Yes.' And knew there was nothing else I could say. Again I was convinced guilt was written all over my face.

For the next twelve months I saw Trixie many times and on each occasion I yearned to be with her, not Gay. I knew I could not change the situation and that the chances of Trixie being prepared to steal me from Gay, even if she had wanted too, were probably zero. So that was how it stayed, me dating Gay but always longing to be with '*my little sister.'*

Identical situations to this arose on numerous other occasions. When I was dating Jen we used to visit a friend of hers called Jane who lived above the 'Bunch of Grapes' pub in Knightsbridge. One of Jane's flat mates was Sally. Every time I saw Sally and her magnificent bust and long legs, my eyes and my thoughts were only for her. A few years later I met another gorgeous young lady with a younger sister called Evelyn. Again the same thing happened: I was dating the older one but madly 'in love' with Eve. By now, though, I was drinking heavily and when drunk, made unsuccessful passes at her all the time.

I kept asking myself, 'Why does this keep happening to me? All my friends are finding one girl, settling down, getting married, buying a house and having children.'

It was as if I suffered from an insatiable disease. I was never *satisfied with what I had got and was* always *wanting someone or something else. In my recovery from drugs and alcohol I labeled this the* 'grass-is-always-greener syndrome', *and I realize that I had it in abundance!*

*****

One Saturday I was as chuffed as I could be when Michael rang and said, 'Jack I'm taking you down the King's Road and we are going to buy you some proper 'gear'. I'll pick you up in an hour.'

He picked me up in his open-top MG and whisked me off to one of the most fashionable King's Road men's boutiques. He was wearing a beautifully cut, two-piece, navy blue, wide-striped, double-breasted suit. With it he wore a Windsor-knotted, royal blue silk tie and a salmon pink shirt. He looked terrific *and I was going to look like this too*!

By now I was also trying to copy the way he spoke. He had the most affected English public school accent I had ever heard, with an even more cut-glass accent than Slim's. And with huge arrogance he seemed able to get away with anything. He was the 'life and soul' wherever he went. He told very funny jokes and did so with a style and panache I yearned for. He had a penchant for Bob Newhart and could recite several of his well-known sketches such as 'The Driving Instructor', 'Sir Walter Raleigh' and 'The Khrushchev Landing' by heart. Needless to say, he was a smash hit with the grooviest of the middle-class girls we met: they all seemed to fall at his feet.

Oh did I want to be just like him and have ALL that he had! ENVY had always been one of my worst character defects and with Michael I certainly had it, but somehow it was not painful. The difference was, with him I was full of gratitude for his taking me under his wing and so for once, I had little or no *resentment.*

We looked at several suits until the assistant produced a thick, black, woollen 'single-breasted', with a one-slit vent. It was extremely heavy and reminded me of my old police uniform – especially the trousers, which were almost identical! Had I really come that far? Flared trousers were in and I was told, 'This pair is cut to perfection.' To go with it I bought a salmon pink shirt like Richard's and a predominantly red, floral tie.

Richard said, 'You look terrific!' And that was how I felt, too, immediately he said it.

Even though it was a hot evening, that night I put the new clothes on and I must admit I again thought I was the bees' knees. I must have looked at myself in the mirror, tying and retying the tie, for over half an hour before I finally ventured forth to the party where Michael was taking me. Here I met Gay and so now I knew *it* worked: all I had to do was talk with as plum an accent as I could muster, wear a slick suit and I could pull the best girls in town too!

Every Saturday night for months after, whenever I wore the complete ensemble, I thought I was as smart as anyone on the block. The madness was that I even wore the clothes on all the hottest summer nights - anything to impress the girls! It was the only trendy outfit I had or could afford; also I did not have the courage to try choosing anything like it by myself.

At last there were several factors in my life that made me feel good about myself. But little did I know that however I looked on my outside, or whatever woman I had on my arm, they were never going to be enough to repair the *damage* that was so well embedded on my inside! I knew the truth about me and nothing could remedy that, *and I always got bored.*

After my relationship with Gay ended, I decided freedom with girls, '007' style, was the only way forward. I was suddenly fixed with a new false confidence and equally twisted mentality towards reality.

I soon had several new girlfriends. One was from Manchester and another lived in Brussels. I used to send them open train and plane tickets paid for by the firm whenever either came to stay with me. Needless to say that as well as being stupid – I was always going to get found out – this was grossly *dishonest.* I was caught and called into my sales directors' office and warned as to my future conduct. I tried to lie my way out of my predicament and was given 'one more chance'.

What I find unbelievable today is that I did the exact same thing just a few months later! By then I just did not seem to care, and looking back, I wonder if my *dishonesty* had gone so far that I hardly knew the difference between truth and untruth, fiction and reality; my mind was in such a mess.

But I did not like it when I was given instant dismissal: 'You are fired!' he had said. This was a huge blow to my *pride, ego* and *self-esteem,* and only the bottle and many drugs were going to see me through this.

It was as if though I had a Guardian Angel. I immediately struck lucky. I had another girlfriend in London, a property developer in Pimlico who had plenty of money, doted on me, lived with her daughter, nanny and housekeeper, and was happy to look after me through such a wretched period. My 'Poor Me' blues were quickly drowned in alcohol and the seeming generosity of this blond, Nordic angel. I did not figure there would be a price to pay for this instant bonding a few months later! As the saying goes, 'There are no free lunches.'

For pocket money I signed on the dole for the second time. The first had been after my father's heart attack several years earlier. The stigma of the dole queues and receiving my weekly benefit were further blows to my *pride:* however, as my alcoholism and drug addiction progressed over the next ten years, periods like these were to become a routine part of my life. As I saw it, the dole and my relationship were the problem, not the booze and the horrendousness of the low moral values I was now living by. *And* there was much worse still to come.

To support my income I decided to become a ticket tout. Andrew Lloyd Webber, Tim Rice musicals and the Royal Shakespeare Company's 'Nicholas Nickleby' were all the rage. I knew 'Joseph and His Amazing Technicolor Dreamcoat' and 'Jesus Christ Superstar' were sellouts, with tickets being sold on the Black Market at highly inflated prices, so I decided to cash in. As I saw it, all I had to do was get tickets for the next sure fire West End hit and I was on my way to a small fortune too.

The new Rice/ Lloyd Webber musical 'Evita' was about to be launched. I applied for batches of two tickets spread across the first eight weeks and got them all. There were rave reviews and I was cock-a-hoop – little did I know, though, the trouble that lay ahead!

On the opening night I had four tickets to sell. Wearing my best city suit, I stood outside the theatre half an hour before the curtain was due to rise, ready to sell to the highest bidder. There was a big crowd and several other touts milling around. I made my pitch at the front of the queue and ignored the 'competition'. I knew what I was doing was illegal, but I took the view that as I did not look like a tout, I was unlikely to be stopped by the police. After several attempts I found a willing buyer who paid twice the original price. I was ecstatic. I almost skipped with joy at my success as I stuffed the four £50 notes and two £10's into my trousers' pocket. I was just setting off to celebrate my success when it happened!

'Hey you, what the hell do you think you're doing? This is our patch! If you think you can muscle in here you've got another think coming!'

I was terrified! I could not believe it. In front of me, blocking my path stood the toughest-looking fiend I had ever seen. Either side him, and closing in, were three others who looked equally mean. What in hell had I got myself into? East End gangs and the executions of the notorious Kray Brothers were ringing in my head.

I trembled from head to toe and tried to say, 'I'm sorry. It will never happen again. I didn't know. I thought anyone could do it.'

I seemed to be stuck there for at least five minutes before he said, 'Bugger off and don't let me see you here again – ever! If I do, I'll do your f...ing head in!'

I needed no second chance and I did not doubt for one

second that he mean it. I was off as fast as my legs would carry me with my tail very much between my legs.

What I now find amazing is that I could not even do the unlawful without being set upon by those of equally dishonest dispositions! At the time I was just thankful to have escaped unharmed, and quickly sold the rest of the tickets to my friends at the asking price.

Within a few months I could not stand my 'kept man' situation any longer. I had come to loathe my girlfriend, our opposing views on materialism and our way of life together. She made all the decisions that mattered; where we went and what we did. And because of my appalling financial circumstances, *I thought I had no choice*! If I wished to continue to live in this gigolo-istic lifestyle, I had to put up with everything she dished out. In a nutshell, my life as a kept lover was eating at my insides and I had come to hate it.

Our relationship had actually got off to a very bad start without my recognizing it at the time. I was on a skiing holiday in Zermatt with my great friend Chris. To get there we had traveled independently, having caught the overnight ferry from Dover to Calais. I drove through the night with Chris sleeping most of the way. On arrival the next day in this exquisite resort nestling in the Alps below the Matterhorn, we booked into a Supertravel chalet near the town church.

The chalet was full of middle-class English public school types and their equally frumpish girlfriends; exactly the sort I had envied all my life. At dinner each night they talked heartily of the day's skiing, and after wine, port and cognac went to bed at midnight ready for another full day's skiing the next day.

Chris and I were there for entirely different reasons. We

were here for a good time. Lots of parties, alcohol and women - with some skiing from mid morning onwards, on the side. After three nights of drunken debauchery I came down very sore headed to breakfast.

The head chalet girl said, 'You have upset the rest of the chalet and we would like you to leave!'

I could hardly believe it! I thought of myself as meek and mild, well-liked by everyone, when sober afraid to say Boo to a goose. *Surely it must be Chris who was to blame*? But it was not. Due to my chronic nightly blackouts, I had no idea what I was supposed to have done and stood there aghast and six inches tall as my punishment was swiftly delivered. All I vaguely remembered was going around the beds of the other chalet guests, pouring water on them and pulling them out of bed in the middle of the night as they slept!

We accordingly and ashamedly left and quickly found another place to stay. This was actually much nicer, and the lady who owned it, Diana, took to us immediately. Two nights later I was introduced to Margherita.

Chris had said, 'She's a very attractive long-haired Scandinavian blond, just your type. She's here with a friend and definitely available!' Next day we met and he could not have been more right with his description – absolutely gorgeous-looking in a chic, petite way - what's more she instantly took to me, too. I could not believe my luck. For the rest of our stay our friendship developed, although there was always the feeling of something ever so slightly 'wrong' with her in the back of my mind. Anyway, it did not seem too important once I had a few drinks: her looks and affection towards me helped my doubting fears to evaporate quickly. I spent the next two days of the holiday eating, drinking and skiing with Margherita and getting to know her better.

On the Friday, Chris and I set off for Brussels where we were to meet our respective girlfriends. I had met Danielle, my 'current' flame, in a Club Méditerranée on Corsica the previous summer. It had been one of the most 'successful' holidays I had ever had – by now I judged all success by the girls I got off with, and on that basis this holiday had been outstanding.

At this time 'Club Med' had a big reputation for boys meeting girls, and on this, my first Club Med experience, I can vouch for its reputation staying very much intact.

I was meeting a friend there, Paul, but due to scheduling issues we were traveling separately. I was to fly from London Heathrow airport early one Friday afternoon. I proceeded to get well plastered: first in the terminal and then on the plane. At this time I was still terrified of flying and I had taken a handful of tranquillizers before starting drinking as well. I was 28 years old at the time. We had a stopover in Marseilles and whilst on the ground there, somehow I managed to get onto the wrong flight. I ended up in Bastia in the far north of the island, whereas I should have been in Bonifacio in the deep south! In my drunken stupor I realized my mistake and got a horrendously expensive taxi to Santa Guilia, my destination, where I eventually arrived much later.

After 24 hours of settling in I tried to organize a bridge game. By now I was playing bridge almost nightly back in London, and had read in the 'Club Med' brochure that bridge was organized here, whereas in fact it was not. On discovering this, I got permission from the 'Chef De

Village', the club manager, to organize it myself. I placed a sign on the Club notice board, which read: *'Le Bridge 18h00, ici chaque soir.'*

The first evening I sat in an open, empty beach hut waiting forlornly for anyone to arrive. After about 20 minutes my eyes nearly jumped out of their sockets. Walking along the beach towards me, in the coolest bikini with the coolest figure I had ever seen, was the most dreamy-looking continental chick I had cast eyes upon since I had arrived. I prayed that she was heading for my bridge sessions. Fifteen yards to go and she turned up the beach heading straight towards me. 'Salut! C'est ici pour le bridge?'

I gulped. 'Do you speak English?' This sumptuous young lady gave the cutest of innocent smiles, put her head coyly on one side, and with the sexiest of husky, French accents, replied, 'Yes a little. I am Belgian.' I was beside my self with joy!

I could not believe my luck as she quickly told me she was 22 and on holiday on her own. As well as her looks, she was totally feminine, had a great sense of humour and was very intelligent too. We instantly clicked but I did not realize for several days that she had felt this way too (I have discovered since that it is very common for French girls to like English men as much as the latter like the former!). Unfortunately some other bridge seekers arrived and I had to curtail my chat-up. Chantal was a beginner, and as the organizer I made sure she played with me every single hand. I was still quite nervous without alcohol when it came to talking to girls, but thanks to my reasonable proficiency at playing bridge *and my ability to bid in French,* we had got off to a good start. Over the next few days and evenings we got to know each other well: eating, drinking, swimming, water-skiing and playing bridge for several hours each day. She gradually joined me and the group of friends I had made from Austria and England more and more, and let go of the ones she had before we had met. In those days I still had a little patience left, and in this instance it paid off remarkably well.

Another interesting incident had happened associated with my alcoholism the night before I met Chantal. It was our first night and Paul and I had got drinking with some other English young men in the bar; needless to say I had got well and truly 'smashed'. The next day we had a late breakfast with them. About half way through, Paul suddenly said, 'Did any of you hear any strange animal sounds during the night?' Club Med at the time had made its model around the straw hut villages of Polynesia and, except for the barest of walls and straw roofing, they were pretty much open to the elements.

Everyone said, 'No' Paul added, 'I was quite frightened by the most extraordinary, loud grating noise coming from outside the wall near Jack's head.' I did not say a word, for I instantly knew what it was! It certainly was an animal all right – it was me! For several years I had had complaints from girlfriends about grinding my teeth whilst I slept. Apparently the sound was horrendous and it was impossible to make me stop. The problem was, in each instance, I was almost unconscious from the amount of alcohol I had consumed and nothing less than an earthquake would have woken me up. I sat there in silence and when I had the opportunity I told the truth to our new drinking companions, but not poor Paul, who had the unfortunate experience of sleeping in the same room as me for the rest of the week. He brought the subject up once more a few days later, but by then the interest in terrifying wild animals had waned and the subject was quickly changed.

Just to show I was not all bad at this time, another interesting development took place as a result of something good I did on my second day. It was about 4 pm and I was walking along a footpath back to my hut. Just in front of me was a woman, a child and a young lady walking in the same direction. They had clearly just arrived as they were carrying lots of luggage. I offered to help, did so, and walked with them to their huts, which it turned out were close to mine. They told me they were a mother, daughter and au pair who had just arrived from Munich. As the latter was quite young, I did not really take too much notice and mostly talked to the mother.

In those days Club Med offered a 'Pacific Islands' style of living. Their guests they called 'Gentile Membres' - GM's - and they all stayed in straw huts, two to a room: the staff were called 'General Organisateurs' 'GO's'. The currency was 'beads', which were only needed to buy drinks at the bar; everything else was included and equally available to everyone. No one was treated better or worse than anyone else. All in all it provided for a wonderfully relaxed way of life. The whole emphasis of their holidays was for people to live together and get to know one another as well as possible in the shortest possible time. Communal everything was the common theme. Everybody ate together, played together, did sports together, danced together, swam together, went on excursions together, listened to classical music together, and so forth. The average age was early to late twenties and a reputation for hedonistic living was quickly established. Each club, and by then there were many scattered across many of the most exotic beach and ski resorts known to man, attracted people from all over the world. It was a truly cosmopolitan life.

The funny thing was, as the years rolled by I continued to use their holidays regularly. The 'free love' lifestyle has long been replaced with family themes, and it seems to me now that just as Club Med had to grow up to survive, I needed to do the same as well. Both of us, because of the simple necessity of needing to carry on existing, had to make major adjustments to the way we played out our roles in life. Club Med had to bring in a 'Company Doctor' to remedy its ills in the 1990's; in the eighties I had needed drastic, life-saving resuscitation as well.

If Club Med's communal way of living and equality of lifestyle were translated today into the Big World with only a few minor adjustments, I believe it would provide mankind with the formula for a 'way of life' we all truly desire. As I have holidayed with them on many occasions - at least half of them in my clear-headed, sober years - I feel totally confident in my analysis: but just like an ex- drunk, it is as hard for Club Med to throw off its wayward reputation as its maligned past!

My first Club Med 'hung over' morning had been a bit of a shock to my reserved British way of life. I had not bargained for its communal bathing policy! However the very next day I discovered the full advantages of this. That particular morning, after adjusting my bleary eyes to the light, I became aware of a tall, long fair-haired young lady standing behind a corner of one of the huts surrounding the area watching me. Within seconds she was by my side washing in the next wash-hand basin to mine. I quickly recognized her as the au pair from the night before, but I very deliberately pretended not to see her. Later that day, as I approached the beach bar, a similar thing took place as she suddenly appeared directly in front of me as if from nowhere. This happened again just as I was leaving from dinner with my group of friends. This time I said, 'Hi', and we chatted for a few moments before I proceeded to the bar. When she did her conjuring act twice more in the next 24 hours I realized she had flipped for me. As a result I started to talk to her a little more, but not enough to call it a chat-up; I saw her as being just too young, and by now I had seen quite a lot of the equally lovely but much more mature and stylish, Chantal. She told me she was American and just 18 years old; she had classic Ivy League looks and a fine, youthful figure. Though she was a bit 'Mid-Western' naïve, seemingly quite innocent, but all too much available to a man who loved a challenge!

By the third night we were decidedly friendly and had an early evening drink together. I had the impression she would do almost anything I suggested, as it was obvious she was completely smitten with me. Consequently I persuaded her to enter the Club Med beauty competition. Of course she won, and as a consequence I started to take a lot more interest in her, as did many of the other young male studs too – nothing like a little competition to grab my attention! Her looks and newly-found fame were good for my *ego* but her age still definitely was not. That night, under the stars and after quite a lot to drink, I tested my suspicions. I found I had 100% accurately assessed her feelings towards me. I also discovered that maybe she was not quite that innocent after all! The trouble was, Chantal had several times more of that which I sought and offered the ultimate challenge. Though had young 'Miss America' been two or three years older, I suspect I would have had a lot more trouble deciding, for she really was a true beauty in the making.

During the holiday I did not have sex with either 'Miss America' or Chantal, but by the time I left, Chantal and I were arranging to meet in Brussels in the next few weeks. Regrettably I had to say goodbye to 'Miss America', who was returning to Germany with her family, and I have wished ever since I had not let her go quite so easily. It was mostly our ten-year age gap that had made the difference, and only a few years on I would have given a lot to be doted upon by someone so lovely.

I adored Chantal in many ways. Most of all she was fun, intelligent, and had the most voluptuous, willowy figure I had ever seen. In the next few months we constantly communicated and went back and forth between our respective homes in London and Brussels having lots of fun. New Year though, was a disaster. I had gone to see her for a long weekend. On the first night we went drinking in several bars, ending up around midnight in a nightclub where we planned to eat and dance. I was, as usual, quite drunk and naïvely ordered steak tartar. I had never eaten raw meat in my life, and due to my inebriated state had no idea that that was what I had ordered! – 'minced beef and chopped onions' had sounded good to me!! Little did I know what lay in store!!!

The next day, I had chronic diarrhea. On the first occasion I had it in the most embarrassing way possible! I was walking along a street with Chantal when suddenly it hit me! I had not, as far as I can recall, ever been more embarrassed in my life. Fortunately I was wearing a coat, started walking with my legs together, and just made it to a nearby restaurant toilet before the next attack came on. I came out a few minutes later but did not have the courage to say what had happened. I just muttered rather pathetically, 'I don't feel very well. I think I'll go back to London.' The real truth was I was consumed with shame and could not stand further blows to my *pride*. I caught the first train I could back to London. God knows what Chantal must have thought, but I was groveling with *self- pity* and felt too dishonored to stay and find out. Quickly, Chantal forgave and forgot and we were back on track in no time at all.

***

Little did I know that this après-ski weekend was to be my last with Chantal forever! Two days after I got back to England, Margherita rang. She said, 'I have to see you. There is something I must talk to you about.'

As much as I wanted to I found it hard to say no, though I did try to rather pathetically at first. She asked me to meet her at the Carlton Towers in Knightsbridge after work 'for a drink'. My fears said, 'Don't go. I am sure she's married.' My lust said, 'Go!' And I did. As a result I made one of the worst decisions of my life and it also turned into one of the meanest.

Chantal was coming to stay the following weekend. She was arriving at Heathrow on the Friday evening and was getting a taxi straight to my flat on Putney Hill. By now I had stupidly got 'involved' with Margherita who, as I suspected, was married. I did not like that one bit, as it was very much against the principles I had grown up to believe in. I had had no encounters with married women before and was appalled at anyone who did – *judging others* had always been a chronic problem for me; it displayed in me an *arrogant* streak, which at times was almost crippling. An 'I-am-right-you-are-wrong, I-know-better-than you' syndrome with which I was well endowed until alcohol and drugs did the 'Humpty Dumpty' on me.

At the Carlton, after some (for me) uncomfortable pleased-to-see-you pleasantries and two quick, large gin and tonics, she told me she was married and said, 'I had decided to leave him before I went skiing …… Our marriage has been over for a long time and I am about to ask him to move out.' I now needed several more large ones to deal with what I suspected was coming next! 'Jack, you are the one for me. I knew it as soon as we met.' As I downed my sixth or seventh the situation did not look quite so bleak, especially given my recently enforced layoff from work: so back to my place in Putney we went. She knew my weaknesses all right, and her irresistible charms and much endearing looks did the rest.

At this time I still had very puritanical views about adultery and marriage when sober, so when I woke up the next day I was devastated; my pride was smashed yet again into smithereens. From here on though, there was no looking back, and Margherita became a permanent fixture in my life as I started to see her almost daily. I quickly discovered I had hammered another of the nails of self-hatred well and truly into my coffin of *self-loathing* and lowly *self-worth*.

A little over a week later, Chantal's next visit was due. As best I could I closed my mind to it and the total mess I was getting into: I was still very much looking forward to seeing her. I just hoped this horrible situation would go away and somehow resolve itself. But of course it did not. The mix of alcohol, drugs and my abominably confused state of mind prevented any logical thinking from taking place.

Margherita was tenacious. She had come around on the Thursday evening demanding I cancel Chantal's visit. I reluctantly tried to, but her father said she had already left and gone to stay with a friend. At about 7 pm on the Friday the doorbell rang; it was Chantal. Margherita had insisted on being there to make sure I did not give in to my weaknesses of sex and alcohol again. She went into the bedroom and I ushered Chantal into the living room. I had never felt more wretched in my life. I was immersed in *fear* and had to have several large vodkas to calm my nerves.

With bowed head I mumbled the situation: 'Chantal, I have met someone else. I tried to call you last night to tell you but I could not reach you. I am sorry but there is nothing I can do about it.' I could not believe I was saying this as it was not what I wanted at all. I wanted everybody and everything to fit in perfectly with my plans, and another wonderful weekend with Chantal was very much part of them. Of course today I can see how pathetic I had been and how my motives were totally *selfish* and *self-centered* as ever, to the core!

I have hardly ever felt more of a piece of garbage in my life. Chantal was dumbfounded and so was I. I am sure she almost knew how I felt. I was ashamed at my weakness, but I was afraid of Margherita and her threat to leave me and that was what prevailed. Chantal hardly said a word; there was nothing to say. I drove her back to Heathrow and left her to board the next plane to Brussels.

On the drive home all I could think of was of drowning my sorrows. I blamed Margherita all the way back to Putney; never once did I think that maybe I was responsible for my actions! My consummate *self-centredness* and *self-pity always* told me it was *someone else's fault.*

My fling with Margherita lasted a year and it was during this time that my alcoholism really took off. Within twelve months, once I had taken the first drink of the day, I had to end it in oblivion. I did not notice it creeping up on me, and why it had to be like this I do not know. To begin with there just seemed to be a continuation of my normal, daily social drinking, except that I always got drunk. Once I had been fired from Colgate Palmolive after a few months of my relationship with Margherita, I became more and more a daytime drinker too. I had far too much time on my hands, was extremely bored and saw no prospects of anyone ever employing me again. It lasted so long because I thought with her looks and money I *must* be happy!

At weekends we went to Margherita's sailing club, and whilst she was off dinghy racing for several hours I sat around the clubhouse drinking. Her husband and little girl were usually there as well, and the tension around that only added to my misery. 'How can so many horrible things be happening to a nice bloke like me?' I thought. 'What am I doing wrong?' All in all this was one of the unhappiest periods of my life. Needless to say, I found in it a thousand and one reasons to drink and take drugs!

***

In all my drinking and drug-taking years there was one girlfriend who stood out, and lasted longer, than all the others. I saw her for the first time at Campden Hill Lawn Tennis Club. I was aged 31 and by now had had lots of girlfriends. All I had needed was one glimpse to know she was the most desirable female I had ever set eyes upon and that, geographically, she was distinctly within range.

It had seemed an ordinary mid-week evening as I walked along the pathway between some tennis courts. As usual I was trying to balance two pints of lager, a box of tennis balls and my tennis racquet, plus sports bag, without spilling a drop. This was taking up most of my attention. As I surveyed the courts for the love of my life for the 1,000[th] time in my six years of membership, there she was: a woman with a figure to launch an armada for. There were no angles missing, she had them all! Her medium-length blond hair, lovely face and curves aroused every feeling of manhood I knew I had and many more I had no idea about. She had the face of Greta Garbo and the figure of Marilyn Monroe. I stopped and watched for a few moments; long enough for her to notice but not too long for her to see it as a 'mind-boggling' stare: though that is certainly what it was! Her tennis did not match her physique but that was the last thing on my mind. Here was femininity to write home about all right, but how to find out who she was? I made sure I played on an adjacent court and could not take my eyes off her throughout my match. I did not know too much about the girl she was playing with but knew I could find out about her as I had seen her around the club: I had done this kind of detective work at Campden Hill tennis club before! I decided I would get down to my research in a week or so.

My almost nightly procedure at this time was two or three sets of tennis followed by several pints of beer in the club bar; a quick shower and several pints more at the Windsor Castle pub nearby. This had become a regular nightly haunt of mine and was one of the socially acceptable drinking joints in town – it was also an excellent place to meet girls, especially in the summer in its renowned garden bar!

I followed this schedule as usual and could not believe my luck when in walked the female tennis player of my dreams and made straight into the bar opposite. By now I had had several drinks and was oozing confidence. I smiled across the bar at her and her look back told me there were possibilities! Minutes later I had changed bars and was talking to her. I complimented her on her tennis which she seemed to find amusing.

Tongue in cheek I said, 'I thought the way you stretched for your forehand was as attractive a stroke as I have ever seen. And the way you bent backwards for your overhead smash defied belief!'

Her knowing smile said it all: she knew it was not her tennis I had been admiring! She bubbled with joy and I was even more enraptured. Here was beauty, wit, intelligence, style and culture, guaranteeing me everlasting happiness all in one hit, I thought - it caused my mind to travel at a thousand miles an hour, never once thinking, 'could I possibly have got it wrong!'

The initial introductions had been easy. Her friend, Joanne, recognized me and introduced us. She smiled knowingly as she said, 'Hi Jack. Good to see you, this is my friend Maria.' My tennis shot volley did the rest and the door was wide open. My very own 'Santa Maria' had come home at last! By the end of the evening I had her telephone number and knew this was *'the one I have been waiting for all my life.'*

I can honestly say I pestered the life out of her for the next three years. Maria was fantastic in almost every way; *but* she only wanted to have fun and be free – bad news for me, as I wanted to possess her. My friend Pete's favorite expressions had sprung to my mind when we met. 'Let me introduce you to a young, blond sensation. Chances like this come but once in a young man's lifetime!' I had taken them literally, whereas he was always joking when he introduced me this way to girls he was chatting up. The more she demanded her freedom the more controlling I became. The more controlling I became the more she demanded her freedom. Winning her became the greatest challenge I had ever known and my sole objective in life. I thought life could only ever be good with her and must only be bad without her. Why could she not see it my way?

Our relationship was on and off for the next three years. In the end I destroyed what I saw as the best *love* affair I had ever had. I was *possessive, jealous, demanding* - and most of all, totally *selfish* and *self-centred*. I either got it all right or all wrong and when things did not go my way I became full of *self-righteousness, self-pity*. My highs were like mountain peaks and my lows the deepest valley troughs. At times she seemed to revel in the attention I bestowed upon her and at others she only wanted to be with anyone other than me. When this happened I resorted to the bottle and drank myself into oblivion and back again. I also drank similarly when I was with her; drinking then at being deliriously happy – with hindsight I see I got drunk on every mood imaginable! Maria had recently been married and now wanted to be unchained. If I had understood this better we may have lasted longer, as she truly was a terrific woman in every way. In the end my possessiveness drove her completely away. Today I am glad to say we are great friends.

When the relationship ended for the first time after just six months, I instantly became harder with women than I had ever been before. I said to myself, 'I will *never* let anyone have control of my life like that again.' This was easy to say but harder to put into practice; though the first time it happened I demonstrated my new meanness immediately.

Maria and I had a date to meet at 8 pm. I rang to confirm it as arranged and she said, 'Do you mind if we leave it tonight? I am very tired and just want a quiet night in.'

I hated hearing this and said, 'What about tomorrow night?'

'Sorry, I am busy. Give me a ring later in the week and we will arrange something then.'

I was beside myself with fury-driven *resentment.* How dare she treat me, the great me, like this? (I have since discovered that *resentment* is considered by many to be the number one defect of character, and that it kills more alcoholics/drug addicts than anything else). I had already been drinking and instantly, venomous thoughts took over my sick mind. Unfortunately I put them into words! The effect was instant. Within another eight minutes she had ended it telling me, 'Never, ever contact me again!'

I was paralysed. Fear seemed to invade every aspect of my body. It displayed itself mentally in acute *anger* and hideous *self-pity.* I did not know what to do. This all took place within no more than ten minutes in a phone box in Notting Hill. Suddenly I had the answer. I would bury myself in alcohol. Never had I had a better excuse before. I knew drowning your sorrows and celebrating with champagne were the two solutions to everything that really mattered in life. I made a beeline for the Windsor Castle pub. Another five pints of beer later I was still seething, but the anaesthetic was working and now the pain was slightly less. By now I was mingling with my usual crowd of male drinkers, but of course I did not have the courage to tell them how Maria had just ditched me!

As frequently happened, just after 9 o'clock, in walked one of the prettiest, fresh-faced young ladies of the 'English Rose' type, with the trimmest of figures - straight from the Lucy Clayton School of modeling – that I and my hoard of merry revelers could ever have imagined. We knew all the regular girls and this was very much a new and lovely face on the block. She was instantly surrounded by several of the would-be Casanovas. I was actually standing at the bar very near where she and her girlfriend took up their positions, so luckily I did not have to move to speak to her. When I eventually did, due to my demeanour I was cool and showed only half-interest. Within another hour I was well oiled, much happier and, fortunately for me, she had decided I was the one she wanted to have fun with.

Prior to meeting Maria, my nightly *modus operandi* had been - after a few pints of beer at the tennis club, followed by several more at the Windsor Castle - to pick up a young lady and take her on to the well-known Italian restaurant 'La Paesana' in Hillgate Village for supper. This I had well tried and tested, and now I applied it to my newly-found friend.

As cool as could be I said, 'I'm off to have something to eat. If you are not doing anything you can come too.' By this time I hardly cared about anything and this came across in the manner in which I made my invitation.

However, my coolness won the day, and I started to think

how I should adopt this attitude to all girls in future! She had had several glasses of wine bought by my competition and said with lots of enthusiasm an emphatic, 'Yes please. I'd love to!'

Tony, the Italian proprietor, was as always in excellent form and said, 'Good evening Signor Ralphs. How are you? What a *g-o-r-g-e-o-u-s* young lady.' He had the most silvery Italian accent and always performed this part of the 'service' superlatively: this time though, it was especially true. For years before this I had eaten there on many nights and mostly with a new date, so I had become a very well-nurtured customer.

In the dimmed half light and now alcoholically relaxed, I saw for the first time how extremely attractive she was: silky shoulder-length fair hair neatly coiffed, big bright eyes, not too much make-up – she did not need any; elegantly dressed and the most frightfully la-di-dah, middle-class accent I had ever heard. I also noticed that she was quite young too. 'What the hell!' I thought, and ordered the usual first bottle of wine: a second followed shortly after and by now we were getting on very well. There would sometimes be a third too, if needed – I never let myself go short in this department, though I often got quizzical looks from my companions as they realized I was almost drinking alone!

After an hour and a half, and much getting-to-know-you lines of chat, I ordered the bill. She had told me she lived in the tower block around the corner and my prospects, I could see, were

looking good.

It was then that I said, 'How old are you?'

'I'm 18,' she said, beaming with joy at the effect I guess she thought this would have on me.

I nearly fell off my chair. I could not believe it and said, 'My God, you'll be telling me next you're a virgin!'

'I am!' She almost shrieked with pleasure.

My *intolerance* took over and I immediately got up to leave. I pulled on my jacket and said, 'I'm going. I can't take any more of this. I've had enough for one night!'

She jumped up and rushed after me. She said, 'BUT I'm looking to change all that!'

After such an offer, what else could I do? I am glad to say we became great friends, have had lots of fun together over many years, and are still very close today.

***

At around this time I became friendly with a married couple, Angela and Bill Mansfield. Bill was a well-established City stockbroker; Angela was a housewife with funny little Shih Tzu dogs called 'Treacle and Jelly'. They lived in a prestigious flat in Ladbroke Square, Holland Park. They were great party givers and allowed the alcohol to flow freely. Regularly on a Saturday night they would organize drinks at their place before going on to a Hurlingham Club, candle-lit supper and dance. They had many friends, most of whom I knew well. These were fun evenings, but the thing I enjoyed most was the constant flow of alcohol, the profusion of single females and the kudos of attending Hurlingham parties that went with it. Hurlingham Tennis and Croquet Club membership was the pinnacle for anyone on the middle-class social scene in London, and I was a regular attendee!

At the time I often commented upon how there were many of our group who were nothing other than 'social climbers'. Today this reminds me of the expression, 'When you have one finger pointed at someone else there are always three pointing back at you!' Nothing could have been more appropriate; that was where I was, all right!

By now I was also playing tennis at Hurlingham regularly with a lawyer friend and at Queen's club - *the* tennis club - with my secretary, Tessa. What was even better for my *ego* was that Tessa became the world number one female Real Tennis player. I also played squash at Queen's Club with Maria's younger sister, Virginia, the number three female squash player in England. Needless to say I was out of my depth on both counts, but in exchange for playing them at their preferred sports, I played squash with Tessa, and tennis with Virginia, where I could hold my own.

Due to my desire for climbing the social ladder, and my belief by now that I could do almost anything, I set off one day to join the All England Club, better known as Wimbledon. Having found it, I was surprised how easy it was just to walk in. Once inside I introduced myself to a young lady in charge of administration.

I politely said, 'Hello. I have just moved to Putney and I wondered if you could help me. I would like to join "the Club".'

She looked slightly embarrassed and, very gently, with a hint of humour, said, 'it doesn't work quite like that: you either have to have won Wimbledon or be invited to join.'

I was quite taken aback, and replied with embarrassment written all over my face, 'Oh. I didn't I know there were such conditions, I am sorry. I play a reasonable game of tennis and thought I could just join.'

She then added as politely as possible, 'There is another Wimbledon tennis club just down the road. You might like to try there.'

I took my exit very much with my tail between my legs and headed for the 'other' Wimbledon club. Here, I am pleased to say, I was warmly received - though of course I did not join: somehow it did not have quite the same ring about it!

I realized years later that it was my ignorance of the 'real' London scene that had let me down. If I had been of English middle-class background I would have known that was how you become a member of this world-famous club. But little did I know what was going to happen next!

I was picked to play for the Campden Hill tennis club bridge team. As a result I did 'play' at Wimbledon, but not tennis! Unfortunately I remember very little about it due to my usual blackout drinking. And sadly I do not even know how many times I played there, as I got drunk on every bridge match evening. We played in a bridge league whose members were all tennis clubs in and around central and west London. Almost every club had a bar and when they did not, I took my own supply of booze. The sessions would begin quietly enough with a few quick 'belters'. As the evening progressed

I would steadily drink an average of one pint of beer every five or six hands for the next three hours. Once the match was over we headed straight for the nearest pub or would go to my home near Marble Arch where I would get totally blitzed. The others in the team, Rodney, David and Michael did not mind a bit and, all in all, these evenings were immense fun. We even did quite well in the matches as well!

By now my Bryanston Court home was always stocked with at least a dozen and a half bottles of dry, sparkling wine. I used to tell anyone prepared to listen, 'My favorite drink is champagne', such was my need to impress. At other times, when desperate enough, I would drink almost anything! Sparkling wine was about a third the price of champagne and at the rate I got through it, it was all I could afford. In fact, by now I could hardly tell the difference and some of the sparkling wines were actually very good imitations. Also at home I kept a full stock of gins, whiskies, brandies, port, vodka, several expensive liqueurs and wines; plus of course 'real' champagne as well.

Chapter 4

A JUNKIE WITHOUT A CAUSE

I continued to confront authority, frequently breaking the law, and every single day of my life my deeply ingrained moral rules for living. By now I was convinced I was the lowest of the low. The word 'sorry' seemed to appear in every other sentence that I uttered. I took on my employers and society at every opportunity: I always courted trouble as my only bride. I could not see that unless I changed my behaviour I would never find happiness, nor that it was the knock-on effect of what I did or said that caused almost all my problems. It was as if I was living in a blind spot in life, the blinkers were down and any intelligence or common sense I might once have had, had long ago gone walk-about.

I got a kick out of taking on major companies in financial legal battles. I won out-of-court settlements from major multi-national firms such as Bank of America, the world's biggest bank, and Xerox Corporation, the largest photocopying firm in the world. On another occasion I had a dispute with a lawyer, took him to the British Law Society and won. I was not afraid of taking on anyone on this type of commercial basis as long as I thought that I had a better than 50% chance of winning. The problem was that each battle took its toll; I became more and more bitter, arrogant, and less inclined to work. No one had ever had 'a fair day's work for a fair day's pay' from me!

Today I know that my legal battles were based on my *resentments,* and were caused by *self-pity, arrogance, sloth* and *greed.* I truly had become a not very nice person to know. But of course, I thought I was being clever! Little did I know that much, much worse still lay ahead!

I started to have more affairs with married women. Each of them was a disaster and they certainly did not help me to feel better about myself! But I still could not see that it was *my behaviour* that was responsible for how *I felt,* or that each of these was fundamentally a sick relationship. I always put it down to the fault of the women *I chose!* By now I had concluded that as long as my girlfriends were good-looking, fun, intelligent, well-off and socially acceptable, I must eventually find happiness with one of them!

Not until many years later did I learn that to have good self-esteem, one has to do estimable things. Where was my brain at this time I now wonder, as it was not rocket science that I was dealing with here!

My thinking got even worse. I tried to use my brain to analyze where my chronic fear of dying had come from. I decided it was because of my upbringing!

I was brought up in a large, six-bedroomed, quite old detached farmhouse on three floors. Often the floorboards and doors creaked; *especially,* it seemed, at night! Alone in my bed, I used to think we had burglars who were coming to get me. Many nights I remember calling for my mother to come to my room to reassure me.

These fears quadrupled when, one morning, I learned that a friend, Paul, had fallen from his

bedroom window whilst sleepwalking. From that night on I barricaded my tiny bedroom window to stop the same thing happening to me. On my dressing table I had a stuffed barn owl in a glass case. Every night just before going to bed, I would jam this into the window frame along with some books, filling every conceivable gap. The window was so small these did the job perfectly. I did not tell anyone about my anxiety or what I was doing to fix it – I was afraid of what people would think of me. The owl had actually been the unfortunate accident victim of a train my grandfather had been driving: now it was being put to a more practical use - to save me falling to what I thought was certain death! At the same time I put bolts on my bedroom door to stop the aforesaid burglars entering. Now I was barricaded in, front and rear, but still felt afraid: and all this chronic *fear* of dying at the age of thirteen! Not exactly the sort of courage a future 'officer of the law' needs when patrolling the streets at three o'clock in the morning! (I have to admit that my courage had not improved one jot by the time I was a patrol policeman either).

Today I see that the hiding of my *fears* was *dishonest* and that it was closely allied to my *pride*. The *'what-would-other-people-think-of-me?'* syndrome by now had a stranglehold on almost every action that I took and the way that I looked. This stayed with me for all my drinking and drugging years and caused me much self-loathing, as each episode in my life took its further toll on my never-ending spiral downwards into the self-made abyss of hell.

Another incident that had a huge impact on me, adding even more to my *fear* of dying, happened on a family picnic. My father and mother had taken my sister and myself whinberry picking on Brilley Mountain, in the local Welsh hills. It was a lovely sunny day, the heather was out and in the slight breeze, and after a good lunch I had lain down and fallen asleep on the grass. The last I remembered were skylarks calling, bees humming, a soft, warm breeze on my face and a feeling of tranquility as I drifted off into the wonderful world of never- never land.

Suddenly I heard my sister screaming!

'R O B E R T, W A K E U P! There's a snake on your leg!' I awoke abruptly and there it was, the most eerie serpent I had ever seen.

I was wearing short trousers and *I was terrified.* I leapt to my feet in sheer panic, brushing the snake brusquely with my hand and arm as I did so. It fell off and quickly beat a hasty retreat into the heather. For years after that I had snake-infested nightmares: hundreds of them chasing me and always at precisely the same location. This was on the main road, just below Glasbury's St Peters church – where, ironically, poisonous adders had been seen in the graveyard's long grass on numerous occasions! I had been told about them on various occasions but never once seen one for myself, though I did see a legless lizard there on a recent visit to my father's grave.

I have never fully got over this phobia, though some therapeutic snake-handling at London Zoo nearly twenty years ago has helped diminish my anxieties.

Linking these incidents to my already well-established fear of dying helped me later understand what a large part this fear played in my overall terror of entering the after-life. If there was a hell, and it was worse than this, no wonder I needed booze, tranquillizers and sleeping-pills to get by!

On two occasions in my recovery from alcoholism the fear

of snakes came back to haunt me. The first time was when I had gone on a trekking holiday for a few days in the Amazon jungle. Within just a few metres of stepping off the boat I was looking behind every tree and bush for the dreaded demons! But worse was to come. We slept in hammocks strung between trees with only the sky above the canopy of leaves. It was pitch black. I have never known black like it before or since, there was not a glimmer of light anywhere. There were nine of us including our two guides and I made sure I slept with someone on all four sides of me.

I did not sleep a wink. All night I lay there imagining a snake slithering down to my hammock and taking a bite! There were many jungle sounds and each of them echoed 'Danger!' in my brain: was it to be a black panther or a snake's venom that would take me to the hereafter? I have never been more awake in my life, or afraid for so long. That night seemed to go on forever.

The worst part was when I had to climb out to go to the loo! I was an average athlete at the best of times but getting in and out of a swinging hammock in pitch dark is no joke. And where to pee – God forbid if 'it' bit me on the willy! Needless to say I survived and did not see a single snake during the whole of the time I spent trekking there!

The other instance still causes me great shame as to my manliness. I was on a playing field with a young child and his ball. I adore children and this child was particularly dear to me. The ball went under a raised platform which was surrounded by grass about a foot high. I took one look and knew I was not going to get it. I was about five years sober but my *fears* had not subsided: 'Snakes!' I thought. The playing field was in the middle of a small town and the chances of a snake being there would be many millions to one but I would not get that ball for all the money in the world. I let the child do it - I have lived with the *guilt* ever since; and I certainly did not tell his mother!

My chronic *fear* of dying seemed worth delving into further; so that is what I did. I remembered that when I was twenty-three my father had a heart attack and nearly died. I took leave of absence from my employer, Cadbury's, to look after his business. He came out of hospital after ten days and was told he needed about two months in which to recuperate. I had been happily living in Leicester at this time, chasing girls and drinking, when, all of a sudden there I was, back where I grew up in very sleepy, rural Wales; not where I wanted to be at all!

One evening, he, my mother and I were watching television. The news had just finished when suddenly he cried, 'Oh God, I'm having a heart attack!'

We were as frightened as he was. I called the doctor whilst my mother tried to calm my father down. The doctor quickly came and assured him he was okay and that it was just his imagination. He gave him lots of sedatives to settle his nerves and something called warfarin used in 'rat poison' that would thin his blood!

From then on these imaginary attacks happened regularly. It quickly became obvious to me that he was actually fine, that he was not having a coronary, but getting better all the time. After a number of these incidents, due to my own fears related to these events, I started to get annoyed with him 'for frightening me so much!' This developed into a form of loathing towards him on my part. These experiences had a profound effect on me as I developed the same irrational fears a few years later.

In fact I was to become a bigger *coward* than my father ever was. Some twelve years later, after evenings of heavy drinking and drug-taking, I would sometimes find I had not taken enough mind- altering substances to put me to sleep. I would lie in bed, certain that I was about to have a heart attack at any moment. I would then get up, take another sleeping pill and drink more wine until such time that I passed out as usual.

***

The reason I had moved to Leicester was because of falling in love with Linda. Linda was a student at Leicester University studying geography. She was tall, slender, with long black hair; a virgin, had an infectious smile and looked like a photograph of my hero 'Slim's' girlfriend. We met at a Birmingham University dance and from the moment I set eyes on her I knew she had to be mine. She was exceedingly attractive and had lots of very nice girlfriends whose boyfriends were almost all good drinkers. They were also all university students. This attracted me, for with my 5 'O' levels it seemed a big step-up on the social ladder. My journey, I thought, had at last just begun. Little did I know that even they would not be good enough for me in a few years' time, given my newfound devotion to social climbing.

I got on particularly well with one of them, Gerry. He and his twin brother Jim were from King's Cross in Central London. They were both good sportsmen and very entertaining in a rough-edged sort of way. Gerry was the most successful womanizer I had ever met. Every girl he wanted seemed to take pity on him and swooned at her first glimpse of his mischievous, doleful eyes. I discovered that his parents were dead and I think the pity had something to do with that – they all wanted to mother him. I could not see the big attraction and definitely did not want to mother him, but successful he certainly was and I thought that some of his success might rub off on me. And occasionally it did.

Linda, Gerry and the rest of their crowd were almost all working-class and very much my kind of people. I really liked them; but when the time came in 1969 I had to let them go, since they no longer met my newfound aspirations for social status. I was not proud of this aspect of my character but I really thought that those with money who had been to public school were happier than those without and who had not. How wrong was I going to be proven to be!

By now I was living in a mews house in Hyde Park Gardens in Central London. During my first year in the Big City I had lived in socially down-market Finsbury Park, in north London. In that year I had mostly socialized with my Leicester University chums, but through moving in with four guys with very English cut-glass accents, quite subconsciously I was manipulating my social playing field. The four were James; a stockbroker, Nathan; a lawyer, Alan; in advertising and Donald; in computers. They lived in a different world to that which I was used to.

For the first time in my life I was totally ashamed of my working-class upbringing and quickly learned to embellish it. For example, my father had adored salmon and trout fly - fishing on our local river. The Wye was renowned for the quality of its salmon and my father was an expert fisherman. But the truth was that he was so expert that he was paid as a 'gilly' to teach the rich where and how to salmon-fish! As I tried to impress my newfound 'friends' I deliberately left out this latter part when describing his livelihood, as I knew its significance. For similar reasons I made up other stories about my upbringing as I went along, leaving out completely that I had been brought up by village shopkeepers! *My whole life by now seemed to be one lie piled upon another to hide who I really was.*

Cricket and rugby are two of the great snob-rated English public school team sports. I was useless at the latter due to sheer cowardice, whilst I had actually been very good at the former. Aged twelve I was picked to play for the school cricket team and had 'outstanding on the cricket pitch' written by Mr Gomersall, our games master, on my school report. Ridiculously I pretended not to like cricket as, in state schools in Wales it was considered to be a 'sissy's' game, whilst rugby was for 'men'. The truth was I had played so much in my childhood that I had actually become both a reasonable batsman and quick bowler. In London I embellished my abilities at both 'rugger' and cricket to extraordinary lengths. I told anyone who was prepared to listen that I had trials for Worcester County Cricket Club and been accepted but that I had turned them down!

Upon reflection I wonder if any boy on the planet would turn down a professional sporting career to become a policeman. That is how ridiculous my story must have sounded but I persevered with it, along with many, many more *dishonest* fabrications.

The next 16 years of my life in London took me from low down the social order to somewhere around middle. On the other hand, on the scale of happiness I went from somewhere in the middle to the bottom of the heap. What I did not notice during this time was that synchronously, my daily intake of alcohol and prescription drugs was increasing year in, year out. It was hard to see when viewed on a daily basis, but reviewing the bigger picture scaled it up its true extent.

To summarize, by now I absolutely loathed myself. I believed myself to be physically inadequate and weak-minded. I told lies, cheated and stole at every opportunity, and I was terrified of dying. There was not one part of me I liked, and most of this by age 17! I was plunging in one straight line of descent into chronic alcoholism and drug addiction, but I could not see that. The way I thought about myself, I suspect, would have driven anyone to drink!

***

There is one other fact I need always to remember. Deep down inside, I always thought I was good, and really just a little boy who needed much love - one who had never grown up. This became even more evident when I was 39 and at the lowest point in my life.

By now I was unemployed, had been arrested five times and hospitalized four times for alcoholism. I still had my flat on Wigmore Street, even though my official home was in St John's Wood. By lunchtime every day I would start drinking. I was full of sadness for myself and loathing for my parents for having conceived me. These thoughts were exaggerated once I had two bottles of wine inside me; then I would walk up and down the corridor of the flat cursing them out loud.

'What right had you to bring me into a world where I would suffer so much pain without asking my permission?' And I believed that in dying there was much worse to come!

I repeated this to myself and out loud, daily. It was then that I would sometimes hear a small, gentle voice in my head saying: 'You are a good boy, you are not bad.' I had no idea where this voice came from as it was so alien to what the rest of what my head was telling me. The voice was full of love and seemed to tell me that under all the veils of hopelessness was a child of the universe, and worthy of much tenderness. And in those latter months of despair it happened often enough to give me just a little hope.

Chapter 5

MY ALCOHOLIC, DRUG DEPENDANT YEARS

For many years I enjoyed alcohol and the effect it had on me. It removed my natural gloomy outlook upon life and gave me courage to do things that terrified me. Although I kept hearing it was a depressant, which took me years to understand, *I knew, for me, it was a mood lifter* and therefore good for me! How wrong I was going to be proved to be!

I took alcohol and drugs for everything. From about aged 20 onwards I stuffed myself with tranquillizers, booze, sleeping-pills and cannabis just to overcome this anxiety. For the same reason I was afraid to fly. Before taking off I would take 20 to 30 milligrams of Valium plus several good-size drinks. During the flight I would consume a further one to three bottles of wine, depending on the length of the flight, and further tranquillizers at frequent intervals. After this I would feel confident and able to cope with any crash!

This way of life ran parallel with me for many years, but in the end it overtook me on the blind side, as if I had never been looking. I had learned to use drugs to deal with everything that upset me and to calm my emotions. All the years I was single, before going to parties, discos or on dates with girls, I would drink several large gin and tonics prior to setting foot outside the door. I had heard that the pre-cursor to alcoholism was drinking alcohol alone but I did not let that worry me one bit. I thought I was on my way and I was, in more ways than one! Drinking 'G & T's' was the way the 'other half' lived, and I wanted to be just like them. The trouble was, when evenings ended for everyone else, I would go around drinking the leftovers! Now if you had my aversion to drinking from someone else's glass, you would realise how much of an anathema to me this was. By then, though, I was beyond caring about anything this trivial.

In my earlier drinking years some of my capers were quite amusing. When I was about 28 years old and living near Marble Arch I developed a 'game' that I played by myself. On Saturday nights I would put on a dinner jacket, have a few large drinks and then do the rounds of London's most prestigious clubs. At this time I used to get drunk but not paralytic. My 'game' was to get into as many of them as possible without paying and have at least one drink in each. I used to start on Park Lane, go on to Knightsbridge and end up in Mayfair. The order was due to the geography of the area where I lived, not anything clever on my part.

My story was always the same; I would tell the doorman I was with 'Dr Vaughan-Davis's party' and that I had arrived 'a little early'. It always worked except at *Annabelle's* in Berkeley Square. By the time I got there - I was stupid enough always to put it last on my list - I would be drunk, and my slurred story by then lacked conviction.

The amount of success I had gave me the confidence to try it on a grander scale! I am a Welsh rugby fanatic and I had heard that the press were putting on a gala reception at the Lancaster Gate Hotel to welcome home the victorious 1971 British Lions from New Zealand. The team was full of my Welsh heroes: Barry John, Gareth Edwards, Gerald Davies, Mervyn Davis, Derek Quinnell, J.P.R. Williams and John Dawes the captain. I decided to try my luck!

It was a Friday night. I donned my dinner jacket and downed several large gins. I felt in tip-top condition. The hotel was only a few hundred yards from where I lived in Hyde Park Gardens. I set off with only a few nerves jangling and lots of excitement.

Getting in was easy. There were drinks at a 'free' bar and I mellowed in well. After half an hour an announcement about dinner and tables was made. I waited in the entrance to the dining-room until I could see a table with two empty places. I made my way over and sat down. I did not say a word. I remember noting famous rugby players and their wives sitting with me. And that is the last thing I fully remember!

I am pretty sure I stayed until the end, and I vaguely recall there being speeches. I woke up the next day fully dressed, clutching a commemorative programme for the evening. Without that I would know almost nothing of what had happened: whom I spoke to and what about I have no idea. Unfortunately for me this would have been one of the most memorable evenings of my life but it was in the middle of my drinking career and nothing has stuck at all: except that 'I went, I saw and I conquered!'

Shortly after this my father died. I am not sure what day of the week it was, but I was awoken by my flatmate, Dr Martin, at around six am one horribly hung-over morning. He had shaken me awake and said, 'Someone's on the phone saying that your father has died.'

I clumsily got out of bed with a very bleary mind, took the call and in a very short time I was driving home. On my journey I kept remembering how my father had been an exceptionally kind man, and deep inside I knew we had always loved each other very much. He had been a wonderful father and always treated me with a gentleness that I do not believe I have ever witnessed in any other man towards his son. I never once saw him lose his temper, and with me as a son his tolerance must have been tested to the hilt. He kept life very, very simple, and that, I believe, was the key to his success.

Due to the many tranquillisers I had taken before setting off on my journey to Wales, I do not remember feeling any real sadness, except for myself, on the whole three-and-a-half hour journey! I stayed at home for the next few days with my mother, sister and family to await the funeral, and due to many more tranquillisers and sleeping-pills, I remained very much out-of-this- world most of the time. In fact they provided me with a complete blank about the whole time I was there, except for one thing!

Whilst in the police force, I had been told that when I attended post mortems I should 'touch' the dead body in order to prevent bad dreams. Shortly after I arrived in Glasbury I went to the bedroom where my father lay and stayed several minutes by myself with the intention of doing just this. I also intended to pay my last respects. But because of my fear of dying, I did not have the courage to touch him or even get close to where he lay. I stayed just inside the door all the time just wishing I was somewhere else. As quickly as I thought reasonable I returned to the living- room and lied about what I had been doing.

It was only at the funeral that I actually felt any sadness for my father and mother, and then I felt lonely too, which rather surprised me. Today I know myself to be a compassionate, sensitive person, and without the drugs I would have been a comfort to my family and very tearful myself as well; whereas on the day I was neither!

***

By now I was used to my daily blackouts, though I did not like them one bit. I would go to rugby matches in Paris and not remember anything except the drinking before the match and negotiating to buy the tickets in the bars in the last half hour before they kicked off.

To get in the mood I would start with a few beers on the Champs Elysées. Then I would hop into a taxi and head for the Parc des Princes. First stop was a bar called 'Le Terminus' on the corner of a large square near the ground. I would arrive about two hours before the match. After several more beers it became easy to mingle with the hordes of French rugby supporters, who mostly came from the south west of France where rugby, like for us Welsh, was the number one sport. Being fellow Celts and drinkers they made me feel very much at home, even when I was there to watch England, our joint bitter rivals. By the time I reached the ground I was always well away and would have mixed many drinks bought by my new French friends, to arrive at this state. The French loved me to try their local brews, which ranged from Calvados to fine cognacs in shots twice the size of those served in Britain. They never had to ask twice to encourage me to do this!

On every visit there was one thing that amazed me. That even after a 'skinful' of all day drinking, and even though I was in a strange city, I would always manage to find the hotel or friend's place where I was staying the night! The homing instinct of alcoholics is one of God's greatest gifts;

ask any alcoholic or drug addict and they all say exactly the same thing!

On another blacked-out occasion whilst on a business trip to Milan, I gate-crashed La Scala. I was staying in a hotel near by and as I walked past this world-famous opera house, I noticed what was on and that it was a special performance exclusively for some sort of socialist political party. After eating in a restaurant nearby, and drinking three bottles of wine by myself, I decided to gatecrash it if I could!

This turned out to be easy. During the interval I just walked in, waited until everyone returned to their seats, chose an empty one and, I believe, watched the rest of the opera! Unfortunately I cannot be absolutely sure that is what I did, as all I can remember is getting in, taking my seat and sitting there for some time. I have no idea as to the name of the opera or how much I enjoyed it.

I forgot much of many other memorable moments as well. The next day, after a Saturday night Kensington party, I was told by my barrister host that I had spent a large part of the evening talking to Christine Keeler! What miffed me about this, and still does, is that I went off to the bar and let her go. I could not believe it and still cannot understand my stupidity.

**

Even with all the wreckage in my life, which was so obviously always associated with my alcohol intake, never once did I think: 'Maybe booze is the problem?'

I just used these rejections and every other negative aspect of my life to further drown my sorrows, and blamed girls for missing out on what I thought was such a good thing!

In a similar vein of ridiculous thinking, I screwed up with my lovely French girlfriend Josyane, whom I had been going out with for several months. We had numerous innocuous dates with lots of kissing and cuddling and were ready for 'the big moment'. She was 23 and a beautiful virgin - at the time I still hoped I would marry one! I really liked her and was very happy for our relationship to develop at a snail's pace, especially as I still had so little confidence in my manly abilities.

We had been drinking at the Hurlingham Club with friends and had gone back to my place alone. We immediately went into my bedroom and started petting passionately. We were entering new territory when the doorbell rang just as I was about to suggest that we undressed; I had ascertained in my mind she was up for it! Incredibly I decided to answer the door. It was Mac, a drinking friend. My crazy mind said, 'Play it cool. Have a few drinks with Mac and then go back and finish the job off.'

So I did. Have the drinks that is, but not the job!

An hour and a half later I returned half drunk to the scene of my soon-to-be conquest. Josyane was most miffed and insisted on being taken home immediately. She ditched me after one more drunken date. Would I ever learn?

***

It is my belief that daily blackouts are one of the most common signs of chronic alcoholism. I had them for years, but had not noticed how they had crept up on me. It seemed as though they gradually became normal in my way of life. Usually the part of the day I could not remember came somewhere between the second and third bottle of wine. But they were to get much worse. Some I was happy to have, others definitely not. The ones I was pleased to have, and which were by far the most frequent, would be when I suspected I had done something for which I would be truly ashamed if I knew about it. These were most frequent in the last five years of my drinking.

Another sign of the progression of my alcoholism was 'brewer's droop'. I had never even known of its existence until it happened the first time. Having needed sufficient quantities of alcohol to persuade someone to have sex, I found it highly embarrassing to discover that the alcohol then stopped me performing! This kicked in from around aged 35 onwards after 20 years of constant alcohol and drug abuse.

By now I would often end up in Mayfair or Soho nightclubs after having got drunk and failed to find a woman to go to bed with elsewhere. In these the waitresses were prostitutes who drank champagne with their customers at considerable cost: both financially and mentally! I was always so blitzed when I went to such dives that I was not welcome even by these ladies of the night. I was also one of those who mostly refused to pay, and as payment was usually demanded up front, all I ever got was a haggle about the price! Sometimes this would create a quite dangerous situation when their pimp was called to come and sort it out. I was always terrified of the pimps, as I had heard horrendous stories about what they would do to non-payers like me. On other occasions the girls would take my word that my cash was at my Marble Arch flat and come back with me. Once there I still refused to pay and offered them alcohol instead. Sometimes they accepted and after consuming sufficient would bend their rules and spend the night with me. Mostly, though, I left the clubs empty-handed, went back to my flat and drank myself into oblivion.

On one memorable occasion I remember pleading with a prostitute to come home with me but to no avail. It was about 2 am outside the Mayfair club where I had spent the past few hours. She was getting a taxi and as I was starting to sober up I could see that she was good-looking by my current standards and I was desperate to have her come back with me; she refused and sped off into what was left of the rest of the night. This particular club had well-educated Western Europeans and white South Africans working there, due to the easy money to be made. I found that to talk to they were interesting and were often teachers or nurses back at home. The trouble was they were often so nice and attractive that I wanted them for girlfriends and could not understand it when they asked for money! Alcohol, by now, had twisted my thinking completely inside out.

Two nights later, when already high, I was crossing Hillgate Street from a pub to a restaurant in Notting Hill with an ex-girlfriend Maria, when I saw this same hooker walk right past me. I could not believe my luck, for she looked just as terrific as I vaguely remembered her. I deposited Maria in the restaurant and rushed back to find the prostitute, whom in my drunken haze I was now convinced was the most desirable woman in the world. I caught up with her and pleaded with her to tell me her name.

After much arguing she said exasperatedly, 'It's Santa Maria.'

I was over the moon; I had broken her at last. I thought: 'I know where she works and tomorrow I can ring and fix our first date.' So I went happily back to join my old flame.

The next day around 4 pm, after my statutory two bottles of wine, I rang the club where she worked and said to the lady who answered, 'I'd like to speak to Santa Maria.'

There was a short pause and a few moments later a different female voice replied, 'Who did you say you wanted to speak to?'

I said, 'Santa Maria. I met her three nights ago at the club.'

At the other end of the phone the laughter was spontaneous and loud! It was obvious my contact had accumulated a group of friends to enjoy the joke. Unfortunately it took me several days to realise my stupidity. I still find it hard to believe the depth of my naïvety: 'Saint Mary', indeed!

Little did I know then that several years later this same name was to play a major part in my recovery from alcoholism and drug addiction. As the saying goes, 'There are no coincidences. It's just God's way of revealing Himself.'

The real trouble with sex with prostitutes or one-night stands is the much-demeaning aspect of side effects. Embarrassingly enough, on several occasions I had to visit the Praed Street clinic at Paddington Hospital. It opened at 9 am, and waiting outside at eight thirty in the morning in the main street provided me with some of the worst moments of my life. It always seemed to be raining as well!

The reason for getting there early was to miss the worst of the long queues that formed as the day wore on. I was convinced that every passer-by and bus passenger knew me and why I was there. This, for me, was the ultimate point in my ever-downward journey into becoming a 'low-life'. Never had I felt so humiliated. Once inside, the long waits in the dreary corridors for my turn gave me time to reflect on the horrendous depths to which my life had sunk. As I saw it, there was nowhere further my fall from grace could descend.

Each occasion on which I visited Praed Street clinic was worse than the last. I had heard of sexually transmitted diseases in my youth, but I had never expected to get them myself. Each time I went there I was lined up with prostitutes of both sexes, as well as many other sad, junkie-type people. After long waits and much hanging of heads by everyone there, we were separated into males and females, to be seen by medical specialists. I felt as if I was now so dirty I belonged to a species of sub-humanity

In the hours of sitting waiting for my name to be called, all I kept thinking was, 'What if any of my friends or family ever find out what I have become…?'

By now I was convinced I had become an outcast from society, but what was even worse was that I had become an outcast to myself. How could all these awful things have happened to such a sweet person as me, and all without my permission?

There seemed absolutely no way out. There was, but I could not see it.

***

Extraordinarily, in the years just prior to this, I had established myself firmly on London's social ladder. My friends were mostly stockbrokers, merchant bankers, lawyers, actuaries, accountants and other similar 'City' public school types. At the same time I had acquired leases on properties in Mayfair, at Marble Arch, on Wigmore Street and Putney Hill. I was regularly attending balls on Park Lane; cocktail parties in Kensington, Chelsea, Mayfair, Belgravia and Knightsbridge; dances at Hurlingham; opera at Glyndebourne, the Coliseum and Covent Garden, plus the royal ballet at the latter as well; racing at 'Glorious' Goodwood; cricket at Lords; rugby at Twickenham and tennis at Wimbledon. I was a member of Campden Hill lawn tennis club, the Lansdowne Club in Mayfair and the Ski Club of Great Britain in Belgravia; I shopped at Harrods, Peter Jones, 'on the King's Road' and Bond Street; I ate at 'April and Desmond's' (AD8), 'Julie's' and 'Joe Allen's'; and I had good-looking, model-type, well-heeled girlfriends to go with my lifestyle's ensemble. To anyone on the outside looking in I had 'arrived': *anyone, that was, except me!*

'Why,' I kept asking myself, 'am I so unhappy?' The answer was: *I knew what was happening on the inside!* I knew the truly degrading way I lived my life. I knew that for every visible vestige of prestige in my life I had to enact multiple feats of balance and counterbalance. But again, I never for one moment thought that daily drunkenness, and all that it led to, had any bearing on the circumstances surrounding my much blinkered, debauched life. As it was, I had only a few lucid moments each day, and what I saw I did not like; I woke up with a hangover and went to bed in oblivion. In the middle I was usually trying to mend fences from the previous night's spree!

By 1973 I had found a friend who could provide me with 'inside information' on the stock market. He knew precisely at what time and on what date an announcement would be made concerning company A taking over company B. I did not have much money, but what I did have I applied to these tips of sure-fire winners. I also passed on the information to work colleagues and friends. Suddenly I became exceedingly popular and, it seemed, admired! This had never happened to me before. I was approached for views and ideas on what to buy on the London stock market and absolutely loved this newly-found attention. I read the Financial Times and attracted new acquaintances with similar interests. James Goldsmith, James Hanson and Jim Slater quickly became my heroes. I even talked to stock market Chartists!

Although we knew what we did was wrong, at this time it was not a criminal offence and many in the City were doing the same thing. Stocks flew in value in the days just before a takeover was announced, as investors got wind of the looming bid. There was no authority in place in those days to stop it, so there was something of a free-for-all by those in the know, and we really were very small fry.

To keep in with my friend, I used to give him half my profits. Sadly, the taxman eventually caught up with me and I had to pay capital gains tax plus a fine for my *dishonesty* – this accounted for almost all my personal gains as I was taxed on my friend's payments too. Also by then, I was carrying losses from 'selling short' in the two and three-week account trading periods that then applied. Overall, I lost far more than I made. As always, I had been trying to be a bit too clever and as usual it caught up with me!

By this time, aged 28, I had also discovered that some of Britain's largest insurance companies owned blocks of flats in central London. They were usually luxurious and in highly sought-after locations. I contacted three of them; Legal and General, Sun Alliance and The Prudential. I requested that I be put on their waiting lists. In a short period of time, *each* of them came up with an offer. I took all three, not informing any of them that I was going to sublet.

Suddenly, as well as being an investor in the stock market I was also a man of property! Shortly after this, one of my 'stock tip' following friends offered me his family's four-bedroom maisonette in Mayfair. I could not believe my luck: though I have to say I was not a very good landlord! It meant I could now sublet all three of the prestigious insurance company-owned flats and live on the income. What an easy way to live, I thought!

Unfortunately my alcoholic mind meant that I did not orchestrate the lettings and mathematics well. One of the occupiers in the Putney Hill flat worked out my little scheme and became a sitting tenant. I then had to buy her out just to make ends meet. Half the time I was too hung-over to manage things properly and had empty rooms just because I was incapable of finding new tenants as they were needed. Eventually, though, I made enough money out of being a sitting tenant to have made it financially worthwhile – let's face it, it was hard to fail with such excellent properties on my hands!

At age 38 I was incapable of proper work, being drunk by lunchtime each day. I had approximately £40,000 left. I calculated that given my alcohol and drug intake, along with my chain-smoking habit, the best I could hope for would be six more years before I died. With my almost 'free' accommodation and dole money, I reckoned I could probably make this amount stretch out for that long. I no longer had a car, had a single female tenant who covered all my rental costs and booze was my only extravagance. Except for the bit about dying, it sounded pretty good, I thought!

Legal and General had bought me out and the other two firms allowed me to buy their properties at vastly reduced prices against their proper market values - but even this did not save me from the financial nightmares that lay ahead. Everything I now did was tainted and it was always only a matter of time before my way of life caught up with me.

I had lived in each flat for several years. My favourite was Bryanston Court near Marble Arch; past home of Mrs Simpson of King Edward VII fame. I loved the flat and its location – it gave me 'status', I thought – something I had never had but always sought. It even had a maid's room and bathroom.

Some status! Frequently whilst living there, I would wake up with a different girl beside me. I would have no idea who she was or how she came to be there. I would try to put the pieces of what I could remember back together; but that never worked as I was now living in a daily blackout. I got rid of the girls as quickly as I could, hoping that they would not be seen by the porters on their way out! This behaviour, I was convinced, would ruin my reputation! *As if anyone was fooled - and I certainly was not.*

This part of central London had many singles bars, my

regular routine was to have about two bottles of wine at home before heading off on foot to the nearest; Fino's, in Mount Street, Mayfair. I was usually quite cheerful at this point thanks to the boost to my spirits the aforesaid alcohol had given me. Although I did this almost nightly I hardly knew anyone who went there, as many of the other barflies were loners too. Arriving around six o'clock meant meeting the girls who worked locally, who dropped in for drinks before going home – not usually much good from the pick-up point of view.

Failing to meet someone in Fino's by about 7-30 pm, I would set off by taxi to Knightsbridge, where I would go to Bill Bentley's or Motcomb's before ending up at Draycott's wine bar around 9 pm. As closing time was 11 pm this gave me ample time to pick someone up. In each wine bar I would order a bottle of wine and drink it by myself, unless I found someone to talk to and share it with. The last of these venues was far and away the best from the pick-up point of view. Here there were always plenty of single, available girls out for the same reason as me - to meet someone of the opposite gender and have sex.

Why I thought one-night stand sex would relieve my loneliness I have no idea. My upbringing had impressed upon me that sex outside marriage was wrong, and deep in the recesses of my mind I was still ill-disposed to girls who lived this way; *yet just as I did*! How *dishonest* could I be? If I did meet someone, and to begin with I often did, we would find somewhere to eat and afterwards go back to my place.

If I did not 'score' in the wine bars there were plenty of well-established pick up joints or insalubrious disco-type clubs I would go to once these had closed in my pursuit of female company. These included Morton's, The Alibi, Stripes, and I know there were several others whose names I cannot remember, due to blackouts. Many were in basements and were dark and dingy, others were considered 'smart', but all served exactly the same purpose and contained more or less the same people.

Mostly though, I would wake up alone not knowing anything about events the night before. Usually I was naked and there would be various pieces of paper with girls' names and telephone numbers in my jacket or trouser pockets. Towards the end of my drinking and drug-taking, on evenings that had ended like this with my feeling acutely lonely, I would ring some of the numbers and try to persuade the girl who answered to come and visit me. Even though it would be well after midnight, I am now amazed how often someone would come, often quite long distances, and spend the night with me. There is no doubt there are many people out there, lonely just as I was.

On other occasions, after a failed tour of the wine bars and being very drunk, I would end up in a restaurant by myself. This was usually 'The Stockpot' in South Kensington, which had booths that were easy to hide in. I would sit facing the wall so that I could not be seen and order a carafe of wine and nothing else. After a few minutes I would start to cry uncontrollably. I believed alcohol had me licked and was convinced I was heading for an early grave following a most horrific, prolonged alcoholic death.

The concoction of *self-centred loneliness,* mixed with my woeful *self-pitying fears,* had by now been terrifying me for many months. But the crazy thing was that the knock-on effect was that I would drink even more of the same depressant to try to relieve the dreadful depression that was now with me almost every waking minute of the day! How insane could I be?

Without meaning to, I had embarked on a ceaseless downwardly-spiralling journey into a morass of impending doom by relentlessly applying a way of life each day that took me to a new level of horror beyond that of each day before.

Surely it could not get worse?

***

To add to my misery, I became banned from several of the aforementioned clubs and bars where I had been a customer for years: they were not that insalubrious after all! Although being a frequent habitué of these was not on my list of social successes, being banned from them hurt like hell. Once at the bar or nightclub door I would be turned away, and with much indignation, and more severe blows to my *lustful* pursuits, ego and *pride*, I would go off in a rage to haunt somewhere even dingier that would still serve me; sadly there were plenty such places!

'I told you last time never to come back,' was something that had never been said to me before, but now they were statements that seemed to haunt me wherever I went.

The trouble was that once back on the streets I was headed for even more trouble. If I was in too bad a state of drunkenness the police would be called, and I would be arrested for being drunk and incapable or drunk and disorderly.

These were yet more hideous features of my now shambolic existence, each adding further to the despairing view I had of what future life I may have in store. And with everything closing in on me I knew that very soon there would be nowhere left to turn.

Today I truly believe there is no bleaker world than that into which a practising alcoholic or drug addict unwittingly descends. It has to be the closest thing to hell that exists here on earth. How else can it be described? It seems to the alcoholic or junkie that there is absolutely no way out; every blind alley leads to more misery and each one is riddled with shame, guilt and remorse. Plus there is the ever-present mantle of *fear* shrouding everything.

And the other problem is: *there are no days off!* Why does every day get worse, never better? At least years ago some days at least seemed okay!

Then I discovered that one of my drinking companions of many years had a 'wet brain'! Was this next on my shortlist of things to achieve in life? Back in school my parents had been told, 'He's bright' and I had been put in the 'A' stream of my grammar school – but where was that brightness now? Why could not my intelligence get me out of this, if I had been so darned clever?

And boy! Did I think I was clever! My favourite actor was Nicol Williamson. The film that I liked him in most was called 'The Reckoning'. He played the part of a young, highly ambitious, tough, heavy-drinking, womanising executive and I wanted to be just like him. It was not a great film and not a huge success but some of the lines I thought were classics.

Early in the film he is getting into a lift with the Chairman of his computer marketing company, when the boss says:

'Which floor would you like, Marlow?'

'The top, sir. I'm going straight to the top,' he arrogantly replies, with a drawl that intimates he knows exactly where he is going and what he wants.

Later in the film he beats someone up who later dies, yet he escapes prosecution by the police. His line this time is:

'If I can get away with that I can get away with anything!'
And that was how I tried to live my life too!

By this time most of my friends were out of my life. In most cases I was too ashamed to see them or they had disowned me. Either way it was just more crap in my life to pile on all the rest. The other problem was that being so *self-centred*, I blamed them for *not seeing everything from my point of view!*

'If you were me and had all my problems, you would drink and take drugs just like I do,' was my recurring theme. BUT *looking back I cannot actually see what my problems were!*

I was also terrified I was going insane. The first time this thought crept up on me I remember brushing it aside. After this it entered my mind more and more often, and I started to believe its imminent, one hundred percent reality, as my life kept gradually deteriorating.

The girls I was now meeting I was often appalled to be seen with. Sometimes they would be drunk like me, though mostly they were just not my type (as I realised when I was sober the next morning!) For years I had dated girls because they had wealthy backgrounds and were very attractive, the latter being always a must. But in the end, I only occasionally dated anyone who matched my requirements. In twenty years of searching for the perfect girlfriend, on only two occasions do I remember dating someone with whom I was agreeably compatible on a mental as well as physical level. Needless to say, I blew each of these relationships almost immediately, due to the ridiculously needy demands my alcoholism made on them.

Such outrageous demands were a major obstacle to my not being happy with whom I had and what I received. As a result I was never satisfied; I wanted my own way in everything and when I did not get it, I was sore. I can now see that with these attitudes prevailing, it was no wonder that I was beginning to question my sanity, as my interpretations of how life should be became more and more out of kilter with those of the rest of the world.

One Sunday night I had the shock of my life regarding compatible girls. A few days earlier I had been very drunk and met someone whom I remembered as very much my type: medium height, dark, slim, intelligent, attractive and so forth. I could not quite recall where we met but I was absolutely convinced this girl had what I liked. I called her a few days later and we arranged to meet at my Bryanston Court flat. My plan was to stay off alcohol and only take drugs for the day, take her out to supper and then back to bed. I only stayed sober when I thought there was a chance I had met someone I would like, otherwise I would have several large drinks before we met and a load more after.

All day I was looking forward to the date, when at seven o'clock the doorbell rang. As I answered it my eyes nearly fell from their sockets. Standing in the doorway, dressed from head to toe in the kinkiest all-black, latex outfit was the original 'Mademoiselle'. I did not remember her at all! Her tight black leather boots went half way up to her thighs. Her miniskirt left a gap of about two inches between the hem of her skirt and the top of her boots. Her latex blouse had a deep V neckline, almost to her navel. Her straight, almost shoulder length, jet-black dyed hair and makeup both glistened. And to round it off she wore an open, all-revealing red plastic mackintosh that shone too!

I was terrified, and this horrendous view of where I had fallen to was to darken my memory for many months to come. I had only ever seen clothes like these on plastic models in lingerie shops or worn by hookers in Soho. I had never met anyone in the cold light of day who dressed anything like this and I definitely did not like it one bit. All I could think of was my image as I hammered more nails into my coffin of self-destruction.

Sure she was attractive, but in no way had I been prepared for this. I had taken drugs all day but now I needed alcohol. I rushed her into the lounge and gave her a bottle, a corkscrew and a glass for wine. I grabbed a bottle of vodka and took it to the nearest toilet. I quickly proceeded to drink enough to calm me and only joined her when it had started to work on my mind. I immediately opened another bottle of wine and proceeded to drink that with her, then one more. The rest of the evening I do not remember except for going to an Italian restaurant nearby and getting completely plastered – normal service had returned!

At the time I owned the lease on the flat at Bryanston Court, I also owned the one on my flat in Wigmore Street, which was just nearby. I used to let out rooms and live between the two, having a bedroom in each. I had let Wigmore Street get badly run down, using it as an office and for crashing out. Although it was a valuable property I was ashamed of the state I had let it get into; the furniture was cheap and the carpets were becoming threadbare. There was dust everywhere. Worst of all was the state of my bedroom. It had broken furniture and two cheap beds with mattresses that stank of my stale urine. There was no doubt it was a fair reflection of the state of my life at the time, and every time I went there it served as a reminder to me that there was *nothing* about my life that I liked.

***

As well as my arrests in London and North America I had also been arrested in France. On this occasion I was on a business trip to Paris. I had arranged for a girlfriend, Yolanta from London, to meet me on the last day of a three-day seminar I was conducting there for senior European executives of Bank of America. We were to travel to St Tropez to see some friends of mine. It was around 6 pm and I was waiting for her to arrive at Paris Gare du Nord station. I was early, had time to kill, and got into some heavy drinking. By the time she arrived I was well oiled and bought several bottles of wine to drink on the train. Yolanta was used to my heavy drinking and never criticized my actions, something I liked very much. She was good-looking, had long blonde hair, of Polish origin though she had grown up in London. She had recently separated from her husband and

I suspect the prospects of Paris and St Tropez pushed aside any objections she might have had.

After getting more loaded I eventually found us a private couchette and we went to bed. Some time later several French people tried to move us, claiming we were in their beds. I refused to move. At the next station, police boarded the train and evicted us. As I angrily stepped onto the platform one of them sprayed my eyes with instantly blinding tear gas. The pain was excruciating and I screamed as I thought I had been blinded. At the same time I was outraged, and cursed out loud, as from my point of view I did not deserve such horrendous treatment. It served to sober me up, but we were still taken to the local police station and detained. After some questioning we were released several hours later and allowed to continue our journey.

The events on the train soured the rest of our weekend, as my arrest did not impress my friends in St Tropez. Unfortunately I do not remember anything else, not even how long or where we stayed, or how we got home! But what I do know is that my behaviour put me out of favour with these old friends for the rest of my drinking career. Today I am pleased to say we are back where we were before my alcoholism took over, and even better friends than we had been before.

I was also arrested twice for drunken driving, the first time with a one-year ban and the second three-year. Today I have to admit to realising how lucky I was, as I could have been arrested well over a thousand times on other occasions for the same offence.

The consequences of driving drunk are very scary, but in my

early years of heavy drinking this did not stop me. The worst experience I had without getting caught was on a skiing holiday with Paul, a lawyer friend from London, when I was about 28 years old.

We were staying in a friend's apartment in Sauze d'Oux in the Italian Alps. We had arrived thirty- six hours earlier, having driven there via Paris - where we had watched Wales (or England!) play France - and through the Mont Blanc tunnel into Italy. After supper we had found a lively bar to drink in. After two hours Paul had sensibly gone back to our flat whereas I had latched onto an amusing girl called Mitch from London. She was having boyfriend trouble and wanted to drown her sorrows; I just wanted to drink. We continued our festivities until about 6 am, when I drove home by myself.

By now the effects of my night's drinking were starting to wear off, but not quite enough to stop what happened next!

I parked the car on the forecourt, got out, closed the door and started to lock it. As I did so, the car rolled slightly forward. To begin with I could not understand what was happening. Then, realising it was gathering pace; I tried to stop it by holding onto the door handle and pulling backwards as hard as I could. The weight of the car was easily winning. Suddenly it was tilting over the edge of the cliff with me holding on for dear life before it plunged down the mountain, veering left as it did so. The slope was about 1 in 3 and there was nothing I could do except watch as it bounced its way down the snow-covered rocks, gaining ever more speed until it crashed into some fencing about seventy feet below. The noise was horrible too, and watching its descent in my stupor seemed almost surreal.

It was just starting to become daylight and I could clearly see where it had come to rest. I instantly realised there was nothing I could do about it and decided to sort it out when I woke up later that day. I climbed back up the ridge and there, standing in the apartment block doorway, were the caretaker and his wife in their night attire: they had obviously heard the disturbance. They looked at me in despair as I walked nonchalantly past them, head down, not saying a word. I went straight to bed and did not give the matter another thought until I woke up the next morning.

The next thing I remember was Paul moving around the flat. I lay there for some time gradually regaining consciousness with the realisation of the horrendous event that had happened the night before descending upon me like a great black cloud.

After a while I said, 'Don't look for the car, it's half way down the mountain wrapped around a fence!'

I said it as matter-of-factly as I could. I followed this with a simple summary of what had happened.

Paul was always laid back and hardly said anything. To my surprise he then said, 'And the night before, did you know you drove straight into the garage doors?'

I said I did not and quickly tried to divert the conversation to safer ground. In fifteen minutes, I had had all I could take for one morning and I did not like one bit the implications of what I was hearing. But at least now I realised why the caretaker had the despairing look of disbelief on his face, *especially as this was only our second night*!

The car was a brand new Triumph Dolomite and belonged to my employer. After several telephone calls it was collected later that day by an accident recovery firm from Turin. About half the town came out to watch the spectacle of it being towed up the mountain. To begin with I was highly embarrassed, but then I realised there was a good story here to impress my drinking friends back in London, and I even took photographs to show off the incident! The last thing I thought was that there was anything wrong with me, or my behaviour, I was just high spirited that was all! My only concern was would the car be ready in time for our return journey? Otherwise, what was I going to tell my boss?

Today I find it extraordinary that I continued to drink alcoholically for another five years, getting into more and more trouble, before I realised *I might* have a problem with alcohol. Then another five years followed with even more serious consequences before I was willing to admit defeat. I always thought I would and could stop whenever I needed to.

***

Sometimes drunk-driving was fun. I was at work one Friday morning when my phone rang. "Hello is that Jack?" a sweet, softly-spoken, sexy, French accented voice said.

"I am going to Lille for an architects' conference today and I don't have to be back home until Sunday night!"

Her name was Bridget and she was blonde, slim and 'très, très chic' - she was also married! I had met her the weekend before when she had been visiting London with a friend of mine. I knew her marriage was having problems and we had exchanged telephone numbers. I had not expected anything quite so soon.

I immediately felt as high as a kite and could not believe this was happening to me. I had my ferry booked and I was on it by 8 o'clock that night from Dover. On the boat I bought a bottle of Vodka to celebrate later, whilst I drank beer in the bar on the crossing. En route I had trouble with the lights of my car and could only drive at a snail's pace. By the time I arrived at her hotel I had drunk the bottle of vodka and I was ecstatic.

Bridget, I knew, was not going to play hard to get and would be just delighted to see me! Yet she did not seem so overjoyed on my arrival at 3.15 that morning!

"Where have you been? And look at the state you are in! I was expecting you hours ago!" was her much unexpected greeting.

I guess arriving a) very late and b) very drunk was not quite the romantic formula she had hoped for!

But I was too drunk to care and said, "Is there anywhere we can get a drink?"

With my manner expressing my joy at seeing her, she quickly mellowed and after an hour of relaxing in a bar, opened especially for us, we proceeded to have a wonderful weekend together. Next day we moved on to the romantic city of Bruges and things got better and better. Even though we had fun, I still got drunk each night and she soon started to refer to me as 'my drunken Welsh friend from England'. Short though our acquaintance may have been – just a few months - my relationship with Bridget was one of only two among the girls I dated in my drinking years, which I would say was actually based upon mutual compatibility: and had she been single, I suspect I would have married Bridget.

I was now 30 and for the first time my moral resolution never to have an affair with a married woman slipped badly: even though her husband was gay, it did not sit comfortably with my conscience. Consequently I had moved down another rung on the ladder of my descent into total self-hatred and absolute despair.

Chapter 6

TRYING TO QUIT

Around this time I realised I may have a drink problem. As a result, I tried various methods to stop. Firstly I went to see my General Practitioner, Dr Kennish in Hyde Park Gardens for help.

After the usual mundane preliminaries he asked, "And what can I do for you today?"

I was afraid of him and after much beating about the bush, I said, "I think I may have a drink problem"

"Oh yes, and how much do you drink each day?"

"Between two and four pints of beer on average - but I chain smoke when I drink," I explained, with much emphasis on the latter.

After about 10 minutes of wasting his and my time with more drivelling *dishonesty*, I left with his suggesting that my drinking was fine but that I should cut out cigarettes!

Due to my *pride* we had not progressed beyond the four pints a day. I was delighted with his prognosis even though I knew it was based on the false facts I had provided, and I continued to drink in much the same way for another five years. Unbeknown to me, my decline into addiction had started and nothing other than total abstinence would be enough to halt its downward spiral.

The second time I tried to stop was when I was aged 35. This time I tried group therapy with an organisation in London called 'Accept' based in Earls Court. At my first meeting they wanted me to talk about any sex problems I might have! I thought, 'This is stupid. What does my sex life have to do with my drinking?' and I gave that up at the end of the first day. (My experience now is that their approach may well have helped to identify some of my problems and that my cursory look at their methods was insufficient to judge their overall usefulness in helping alcoholics and drug addicts.)

Shortly after this I sought psychiatric help. I had revisited my doctor and this time told him the truth about my alcohol intake. He referred me to Max Glatt, at the time Britain's best-known psychiatrist specialising in alcoholism. Max understood my predicament immediately and suggested I attend RPNH, the Regent's Park Nursing Home on Primrose Hill in London, where he presided. I was admitted a few days later and detoxified. He told me that I was in grave danger of having an epileptic fit if I came off alcohol 'cold turkey', due to the quantities I had been drinking over many years, so he gave me an anti-fit drug called Epanutin to prevent this. I left a week later and was on the bottle within two hours of leaving. This was though no fault of Max's or the RPNH, it was just that I had not accepted I was a *real* alcoholic!

My drug cocktail was increased on each of my four admissions to the RPNH. As well as Epanutin, I was given more tranquillisers, more sleeping-pills, and for the first time, antidepressants and Heminevrin - a heavy-duty tranquilliser - in ever-increasing amounts on each visit to try to stabilise me. Before I went to the nursing home my body swilled to and fro; by the time I left, it rattled and I still rolled!

I have never blamed the medical profession for my alcoholism or drug addiction, but these were all strong drugs and considering I was admitted to be weaned off alcohol, as strong a drug as any of them in the quantities I drank, it now seems obvious that drug substitution was a futile approach to my problem. To substitute one addictive drug for another cannot make sense; it can only lead to a transfer of dependence, never dealing with the underlying condition. Even though I have not drunk alcohol or taken drugs for over twenty two years, today I know I was and always will be, an alcoholic: though today my alcoholism is latent and very much in abeyance. It was my mental attitudes and back-to-front way of dealing with life's everyday issues that needed sorting out, and what I needed to cure these was a psychological approach: fortunately for me such treatment did exist.

Today there are many agencies trying desperately to offer solutions to alcoholism and drug addiction. Our prisons are well over 60% full with inmates who have committed their crimes under the influence of alcohol or drugs. Our hospitals too, have similar demands made upon them from people suffering with other addiction diseases such as gambling, bulimia, anorexia and sex. So the need for well-informed agencies with tried and tested solutions is paramount. All of these, I believe, are well-meaning, but in my experience there is only one way works and that constitutes the basis of the final chapter of this book.

To an addict, being addicted to one drug is just like being hooked on any other. In my case if it had not been alcohol, prescribed drugs and marihuana, it could have been cocaine, ganja, cannabis, Ecstasy, L.S.D., methadone, 'crack', heroin, glue, 'speed'; any of the other hallucinogenic or psychedelic drugs, benzodiazopines and/or antidepressants or any of the other mood-altering drugs on the market. It was just that I did not try the others, that was all. Whether I drank, inhaled, sniffed, ate or injected would have been irrelevant, it would be the effect they would have on my mind and body that I would have craved.

As a result of my experience I firmly believe that addiction and alcoholism are so hard to understand unless you are an addict or an alcoholic, that until the medical profession has learned to grasp the nature of the problem and the solution it is essential to have recovering addicts involved in formulating answers to the horrendous killer nature of drug and alcohol dependence and addiction. Only then will we fully engage in the battle of combating mood-altering substance abuse, and only then will pathways be opened upon the mountain of criminal, health and financial problems caused by alcohol and drugs. Sadly, the fact is that governments might well listen to doctors and psychiatrists, but it is unlikely that they are going to take seriously the words of ex- alcoholics and junkies, even though they are the ones with first-hand experience of both addiction, rehabilitation and recovery.

Unfortunately, there is still a huge lack of understanding by non-addicts of the nature of addiction. Too often, jobs in the drug rehabilitation sector are given to those without relevant experience. It is necessary to understand in depth why an alcoholic or addict puts lethal poisons into their bodies when they know that doing so will eventually kill them. It is not that they want to take drugs; it is that they believe they have

123

no choice. Also, to believe that drug-addicted people are weak-willed is a misconception - though a totally understandable one, since addicts themselves would have always believed they would one day be able to quit by using their own willpower. For months or years, as their addiction developed, they would have thought along these lines just as I did.

It also needs to be understood that if an addict or alcoholic wants to drink alcohol or take drugs he or she will do so; nothing I know of in this present climate of easy accessibility will stop them, especially as alcohol is available to anyone over eighteen on every street corner twenty four hours a day. This being so, complete prohibition would seem to be the only answer: but that does not get to the root cause of addiction or alcoholism, *that is what has to be dealt with and that is what is most misunderstood by those appointed to senior positions in governments, health and crime services.*

There is also a huge misunderstanding about so-called 'hard' drugs. Ask any addict and he or she will tell you that these drugs are no more or less harmful than socially acceptable alcohol, cannabis or prescription drugs, as simply increasing the amounts the addict needs for a 'fix' from any of these provides the mood-altering effect he or she needs. All you have to do to understand this is to compare the health, attitude to life and demeanour of any down-and-out junkie or alcoholic on 'soft' or 'hard' drugs and they look and behave the same, whatever the nominal category of the drugs that have caused their downfall. Try asking the parents of any alcoholic, valium or sleeping pill junkie, heroin, cocaine, ecstasy or glue-sniffing addict and they will confirm this. Until these facts are recognised by those with influence, no really successful inroads into the problems of drug addiction and alcoholism are likely. Even if the streets were completely free of all drugs other than alcohol and prescribed drugs, and it were made impossible for addicts to acquire their current drug of choice, a shift in addiction to booze and pills for almost all with *'addictive personalities'* would take place. It is the person, the addict that is sick; the drugs themselves are not the problem.

Today many in the medical profession realise this and they now need to point it out categorically and unequivocally to governments and the agencies concerned. Addiction is a medical condition. It is an illness, a disease, and it cannot be treated by other addictive, mood altering drugs. Only total abstinence and a profound mental change of attitude and associated actions will work to treat it effectively. Such a change of understanding could eventually lead to slamming the door shut on drug addiction and alcoholism once and for all.

To glamorise alcohol in advertising, and then perversely to have some drugs classed as illegal does not help or make sense either. To alcoholics, addicts and anyone who understands addiction this sends a mixed, double-edged message. On the one hand governments and the public are supportive when it suits them to be so, but on the other hand the use of other, no more nor less lethal drug leads to imprisonment and banishment from society. Like most addicts and young people I was a rebel: I enjoyed drinking under-age *because it was illegal.* Then later I enjoyed smoking dope and getting 'smashed' for the same reasons. And this attitude of rebellion, in some measure or other, provided much the same motivation for most of the many thousands of alcoholics and addicts with whom over the past twenty years I have had the good fortune to share my experience.

Whilst governments reap huge financial rewards from duty on addictive substances such as alcohol and tobacco, (UK government: £20 billion + and gambling £2 billion +), and pharmaceutical companies £ billions of profits on addictive drugs, there is unlikely to be a sufficient attitude change by their administrators to address the problem.

If you are still have any doubt as to the confusion the world's alcohol and drugs laws cause, it is not surprising, as they leave us asking two seemingly absurd questions:

1. What are the differences between the overall effects of the drugs a hop grower in Kent, an apple grower in Herefordshire, a grape grower in France and a barley grower in Scotland produces versus those of a poppy grower in Afghanistan and a cacao grower in Columbia? (I'm darned if I can see the difference: except you might get killed or imprisoned for life for growing either of the latter two!)

(2) What about pharmaceutical companies? Why are they are allowed to market their products freely when many of them are known to be equally as lethally addictive and harmful as any other narcotic on the market? (GSK's antidepressant Seroxat is a known cause of suicide; and coming off Ativan/Valium and Mogadon/Euhypnos forte nearly killed me!)

So it has to be left to the medical profession and the example of those of us who are recovering from addiction to help those who do not understand to expound the true nature of addiction, its causes and what needs to be done to address its symptoms. And as it took me 25 years of drug abuse followed by 20 years of abstinence to understand my own addiction problem, I suspect it will be a long time before the much-needed changes come into being, as they have to be brought about by people without the life threatening experience I had: or until the general public become unhappy with the status quo.

Max Glatt understood, as do scores of other professionals like them. He understood so well he tried hard to persuade me to go to Alcoholics Anonymous (A.A) for my alcoholism and Narcotics Anonymous (N.A.) for my drug addiction. Both organisations do take such an approach, treating the root cause of the problems. But at the time he suggested this I did not want to know. It was only after I had totally accepted that I was an alcoholic and drug addict that I became willing to go to any lengths to stay clean and sober. And it was such a change of attitude followed by rigorous action on my part that was the answer to my life-threatening illness.

Each time I went to Regents Park Nursing Home I had the same desire to stop. Every cell in my body was crying out for me to quit but I just did not have the mental tools to fight the hold booze and drugs had on me. Each homecoming had exactly the same result: if I made it that far! And with each period of time in between visits, my drug and alcohol problem got worse.

Typically, as on the last occasion I was there, I was met as I left by my then girlfriend Sally, who was totally supportive of my quitting. She had seen the best and the worst of me in our months of dating. When I was sober I was a kind, attentive and thoughtful - though *self-centred* - boyfriend. When I was drunk I was abominable. It was as simple as that.

As soon as we were outside the building I said, "I need a drink!"

She knew there was no point in arguing as she had been here with me many times before, and I dragged her off to the nearest pub where I downed several large gin and tonics. This did not impress Sally or me, and she said as much, though knowing they were wasted words, as nothing would stop me once I reached that point. Incredibly I was still not totally convinced intellectually alcohol was my problem. Deep inside, though, I knew I could no longer face life with or without alcohol and that time was fast running out.

Such were the depths of my fear of dying that from now on, every time I tried to go a day without alcohol - for which massive quantities of prescription drugs were always substituted - I made sure I had sufficient quantities of Epanutin to prevent my having an epileptic fit. I had got to the point where I lived in a state of perpetual fear, and of course this only ever got worse as my daily intake of drugs and alcohol progressed. So by now I had at least one mood-altering drug to take care of every uncomfortable feeling I had!

As well as Max Glatt, I also started seeing another psychiatrist whom Max recommended. Thanks to BUPA I saw one or other of them almost every week. His name was Patrick O'Connor and he also specialised in alcoholism and drug addiction. I will always remember the first time we met.

My appointment was at 10 a.m. I arrived at his Harley Street clinic with my usual howler of a hangover still clinging to my much- dulled mind. His nurse answered the door and I was ushered into a waiting-room. A few minutes later in walked 'Paddy'. He was short, stooped slightly and had a purposeful look.

"Good morning. I am Dr O'Connor. Please come with me," he said so quietly that I had to get quite close to him to hear.

After a few strides along the corridor he looked at his watch then turned to me and said, "You know you still reek from yesterday's alcohol. What time did you take your last drink?"

No one had ever challenged me like this before. I was speechlessly stopped in my tracks as my mind fumbled its way into gear.

"I think it was about 11 o'clock last night," I meekly replied, guessing it was hours later, but not actually having a clue as to when it really was. I thought this would be a good answer from his point of view!

He said matter-of-factly, "It usually takes eight to nine hours to clear the system."

I quickly calculated that my dishonesty had been discovered within a minute of meeting him, and from that moment on I decided that it was best to tell him as little as possible about my drinking habits. By now I knew that the words I used to describe my life were so far removed from reality that it was unlikely he would learn anything even vaguely resembling the truth about the addiction that was crippling me. Why I was bothering to see him, therefore, may be hard to understand, except that deep inside me lived a terrified child longing to be freed from the stranglehold of chronic alcoholism and drug dependency that I now knew I was in.

And that was how my relationship with Patrick stayed for the three years he treated me; he was always at least one step ahead of the lies that I automatically told. He knew exactly what treatment I needed, but due to an absolute denial on my part, I would not follow his recommendations. So for the next two years we went round and round in circles before I finally reached my breaking-point. But that I describe in another part of my story!

Today I see how my attitude to the drugs I was prescribed was deeply screwed up, and the result was to cause me much additional dependency; plus later chronic withdrawal problems. What I was doing at the time seemed innocent enough, though I was not proud of being hooked on 'granny-takes-these-to-soothe-her-nerves' type pills either! After all, one of my main ambitions was to be '*a Man*'. But as far as I was concerned, just to live, I no longer had a choice; the fears surrounding every aspect of my life were just too great. Mentally I tried to use the excuse that 'as the drugs are prescribed by the medical profession, they can only be doing me good!' But I knew this was a lie, as I was not being honest with the medical professionals about how many sources for supplying drugs I had. I just heaped lies upon lies upon lies. And the funny thing is, it is only now in writing this twenty two years later with a clear head that I realise the depths of despair I was in and the chronic levels of *dishonesty* to which I had by then succumbed.

***

Another of both my psychiatrists' suggestions was that I take *Abstem*. This is a substance like *Antabuse*, which is highly dangerous if alcohol is drunk within 24 hours of taking it. I refused to take it for several years, too afraid that I could not stop drinking for long enough for it to be safe - *i.e. just one day!* On my last visit to Regents Park Nursing Home I gave in. The trouble was, I very soon discovered I could just about get away with drinking alcohol the same day, *if I was extremely careful.* For an alcoholic who could not stop after even a single drink, this turned out to be a potentially lethal fact!

In my experience, skiing holidays and alcoholism do not go well together. Regularly I would go with my friend Jonathon and stay in his apartment in Anzere, Switzerland. He was used to my drinking and on one occasion had christened me "'Petrol', because you will drink anything!" On another we had taken a friend's twelve-year old son Toby. On the fourth night, as I poured some early evening drinks, he made the following classic observation.

"You know, Jon, if Jack had a brain he would be dangerous," he astutely said, having seen the state I had got into on the past three nights!

For this latest skiing adventure I had brought a girlfriend, Emma, with me. I was 27 days without alcohol, having filled myself full of tranquillisers, sleeping-pills and *Abstem* to get me through each day. We were in a bar and I ordered a 'Virgin Mary' with angostura bitters. I started sipping it and then I asked the barman about the bitters.

"What's in the bitters? Do they contain alcohol?" I naively asked, expecting the answer to be an emphatic "No".

He said, "Yes they do. We use them to make 'pink gins'!"

I freaked out. I was sure I was going to be dead within the hour. I told Jon and Emma of my instant terror and immediately rushed to a phone and rang my psychiatrist, 'Paddy', back in England. Fortunately he had given me his home number: *"in case of emergencies,"* were his exact words - as if he had known! I thanked God when his wife answered and said that he was in.

Paddy had vast experience of alcoholics like me and was most importantly, and thankfully for me, one of the kindest and most patient men I have ever met. How he put up with the gibberish I spewed forth through our many hours of consultation, year in year out, I will never know. He was also blessed with the gentlest, most softly-spoken Irish brogue, and reassuring manner I had ever encountered: in fact from the moment we met I thought of him as my one and only possible lifesaver; though I did not believe for one instant I could ever be cured. I also believed he had warmed to me too, and for the first time in my life I felt that someone outside my family genuinely cared about me.

"Hello. Dr O'Connor here," he said as reassuringly as ever.

I blurted down the telephone, "Patrick, it's Jack. I am in a bar in Switzerland and I've just drunk on Abstem. What the hell am I going to do?"

He said as smoothly as silk, "Hello Jack. And how much have you drunk, dear boy?" "A Virgin Mary with some angostura bitters," I replied at 100 miles an hour.

"If that's all, Jack, don't worry: as long as you stop drinking now you will be fine," he assured me.

We talked for a little longer but *for now he had given me the answer I needed to hear* and I obeyed his command to the letter. Fortunately for me I had not consumed enough to set off my normal mental and physical craving, even though for the rest of the evening I remained on tenterhooks.

I did not consume another drop of my tomato juice cocktail. I left the bar almost immediately and went back to our apartment where I proceeded to swallow enough of Hoffmann Le Roche's world famous tranquillisers and sleeping pills to put an elephant out of any misery – I was not taking any more chances! I drifted off into a deep coma and stayed that way until mid-morning next day.

The rest of the holiday passed without incident. Within a few days I was back in London where my fears and loneliness caught up with me and the future looked as bleak as ever. I had already taken my daily dose of Abstem. With a rejection of rationality pulsing through my brain, I analysed my situation for the umpteenth time. In every direction I looked the prospects for my future looked bleak. I had no job, few friends, nothing to do all day, a dwindling amount of money and no income: I had lost my driving license and was threatened with prison. My girlfriends were prostitutes or those that I would not wish to be seen with except when drunk, I had had several alcohol-related arrests and four hospitalisations; plus I could see my overall health was gradually deteriorating. There was not one bright spot on the horizon. Worst of all, I felt unloved and that there was no one in the world to whom I could explain my predicament. BUT *I now knew I could get away with drinking alcohol within twenty-four hours of taking Abstem, if I was very, very careful!* So I decided to try it.

Even as I had taken the Abstem that morning, I think I had known I was going to surrender to booze later that day. I could stand the misery no longer, and after several hours of wallowing in self-pity I gave in to the continual craving that was consuming my mind and body.

I opened a bottle of wine and proceeded to drink as slowly as I could. First one glass, nothing: then another, again nothing.   Could   the   doctors have got it wrong, I wondered? Five minutes passed and I was half-way into a third glass. I started to feel my face flushing. At first I thought I was imagining it and went to the bathroom to look in the mirror: I could not believe the colour of the face looking back at me – I looked like a baboon! I was turning crimson before my veryeyes.

I realised my body was starting to feel the same. I took off my shirt; my skin was blotched bright red and this effect was visibly spreading. I stared at myself, totally petrified, not knowing what to do but knowing for certain that I could not stop drinking now that I had started.

For a few minutes I was even too terrified to drink. Then my heart started to beat quicker. It was as if a drummer were inside my chest trying to beat a way out, and all the time it got quicker and quicker. I drank some more, almost sipping by my standards. The beating got sharper and the reddening worsened. By now I knew I could not stop. I kept this up for what seemed like several hours, though in fact it was probably two at the most.

At last the redness started to disappear and my heartbeats gradually returned to normal. By now I had drunk about two bottles of wine. With massive relief I realised I had survived.

It was dark and early evening: to celebrate my survival I went to the dingiest of the wine bars I frequented and more or less behaved as usual until I passed out around midnight.

Next day I did not dare take Abstem and drank myself into oblivion, almost to celebrate my freedom to drink again. Two more horrendous days like that and I was back on it again with exactly the same results. The only difference was, *I knew I could survive if I drank as slowly as I could.*

And that was how my life went on for the next twelve months; always knowing that once I had taken that pre-emptive mouthful of alcohol nothing on this planet would stop me from carrying on until I was drunk or in oblivion, whatever the consequences. Why I bothered to take the Abstem when I first woke up on many occasions I could not understand; it just did not make sense to me at the time.

Today I understand that there are considered to be aspects of insanity associated with alcoholism. One of these is doing the same things over and over again but expecting different results! So now insanity was knocking at my door as well!

I have also since learned that to an alcoholic or drug addict, it is the first drink or drug that does the damage - not the tenth or twentieth as I had always thought!

The progression of addiction is usually gradual. I had doctors, and later both my psychiatrists, prescribing tranquillisers and sleeping-pills for me for twenty years. I took them like sweets. I started taking between 5 and 10 milligrams a day when I was twenty and finished on between 150 and 300 a day when I was forty. By crafty manipulation

I had put in place all the resources I needed to meet the requirements of my daily addiction. None of the doctors knew about the others, so they were not aware of the true quantities I was consuming. One of them switched me from *Valium* to *Ativan,* which he told me was stronger. I had no problems with that: if someone in the medical profession thought it was right for me, then I did too. In addition I switched chemists around so as not to be found out. One of these even let me have pills without a prescription when I needed a top-up. I managed all of this so meticulously that I never once ran out as I learned to balance my act perfectly.

There was one occasion, however, when things badly backfired! Very drunk as always, I had rung the number on one of my 'pieces of paper' of one of the girls I had met on a previous night. She refused to come and see me but said it was okay for me to visit her. It was after midnight and, well armed with booze, I set off by taxi to wherever she lived. *But, for the only time ever, I forgot the following morning's supply of Valium*!

I woke up the next day in my usual state: a hung-over, trembling wreck. All I knew was that I was somewhere in the outer suburbs of North London. I could not wait to get out of her flat, and being in such a hurry, I did not ask directions. It was a Sunday, and London provincial transport is not good on Sundays. I set off walking, hoping to find a bus, tube or taxi very quickly. It was about 11 a.m. and it took me over three hours to reach my Marble Arch address. By the time I got there I was desperate for a fix. My nerves were jangling; I was at my wits' end.

On the way home I realised I could not remember when I had gone so long without my first-thing- in-the-morning

Valium comforter – I started to panic, as Boy! did I now need a fix! For the first time I began to see, but not acknowledge, the mess I was in with prescription drugs: in fact once home I did not give it another thought, I was just so relieved to have the much needed drugs inside me and be back in my safety zone. Never was I going to be caught short like that again - and I was not!

In the years since quitting I have had time to reflect and ask questions. For me, one of the most interesting aspects about addiction to tranquillisers, sleeping pills and antidepressants, especially GSK's Seroxat, the so-called Opium of the masses, is that even when thousands of their victims are known to have committed suicide directly as the result of using them, they are allowed to continue to get away with what to the rest of the world would be manslaughter! As someone once said: "Money talks!"

Other Demons of Alcoholism

Due to the *dishonesty* of trying to hide from my friends my habitually drunken way of life, I still thought no one had any idea as to the desperate state my alcoholism had reached. I knew I had been able to conceal my chronic drug addiction successfully, as popping little pills without scent or obvious physical side effects was easy. I was later to discover that *almost all alcoholics and drug addicts will go to extreme lengths to cover up their substance abuse and that this is just one of their many trademarks.* This only ever serves to add to the individual's denial as to the depths of their addiction, even though they know full well themselves the desperation of the personal circumstances they now wallow in.

In the last few years of my drinking career it became

impossible to hide from such reality any more. On numerous occasions there occurred situations outside my control when I was unable to get away with my deception: in other words, I was found out!

I used to play squash with two friends, Dan and Ray, most Friday nights. Dan was a partner in one of the world's leading international law firms and Ray was Chief Executive of a well-known British public company. I had been playing and partying with them for years and in times long since past, we had had many amusing adventures together – now though, I was just trying to keep the last threads of my tattered reputation intact!

I was in my late thirties and very ashamed of the state of my physical condition: red lines on my cheeks, blood-shot eyes, and my trembling hands were all too clearly visible. I was desperate that they should not get to see the terrible shakes I now suffered when I took the first drink. To try to hide this from them I made sure I always arrived before they did so that I could play each of them first and be off court and in the bar well before they had finished playing. I thought my ploy was working!

As soon as I had completed my two matches against them, I would shower then rush to the bar and order two pints of beer. I would gulp down half the first in one hit, drink the other in the loo where I would have chronic diarrhoea, then speed back to the bar to be there before they arrived. I would then drink the other half pint and order a third so as to look as though I was still on my first at whatever point they joined me. I thought I was being very clever!

Once these 'levellers' were inside me, my jitters eased and I could then drink sociably with them for the rest of the time they stayed, usually about an hour. At this point they would go home to their wives and families whilst I turned into a night owl and went in search of female company in my usual cluster of West End wine bars.

The trouble was that after a few months of this formula as to the order we played, they became wise to my *modus operandi*. One night, after we had a few drinks, Ray told me they had cottoned on to what I was doing. This of course rubbed more salt into my badly bruised, wounded *ego*. After this I had to stop playing them, my *pride* could not take it.

I now refer to these as '*embarrassing moments*'. One of the worst of these happened when I went to an early Sunday evening drinks party with Ray at Davina's, a South African friend. I knew I was in trouble even before we arrived. I could no longer take the first-of-the-day's alcoholic drinks slowly; and he was likely to be with me when I took my '*numero uno*', *quivering, quencher*!

We walked into the dining-room where many glasses of wine were laid out on the table. I picked one up, drank it straight down, then another and another: then I looked at him and caught full on the grimace of disbelieving astonishment that was written across his face. We had done much drinking together for many years, but he had never seen me like this before and he said so.

With horror resonating in his voice he said, "My God! What the hell are you doing? Is this what you have come to?"

"I don't have a choice," I said and looked sharply away. I picked up another and went directly to the bathroom where I had my usual bout of diarrhoea. It was then for the first time that I knew I was totally beaten and that there was no turning back: hell was the next stop for this ex party- loving animal!

The rest of the party I do not remember, but next day I knew it was all over for me with Ray and anyone else he cared to tell. The death-nails were being hammered in thick and fast into the coffin of my social acceptability, and this was almost the last of them – my days of being invited to parties by anyone were rapidly running out. So I gave them myself and hoped that way to fill the gap!

I still had money, 'acquaintances', and my prestigious Bryanston Court flat on George Street. With help from two friends I organised some 'singles' parties where I provided lots of 'bubbly', decent food and music. My motive was double-pronged. On the one hand I wanted girls for myself and on the other, I thought such parties would keep me 'in' with my rapidly depleting circle of male 'friends'. So I invited my married male friends to come on their own, and lots of single, attractive, good-time girls! The parties worked well from the 'my getting drunk and having a good time' point of view but little else. No one was impressed - especially my friend's wives! All I ended up with were big bills, fewer invitations and more sore heads.

Many of the later side-effects of my alcoholism, as well as being embarrassingly visible, were also physically extremely unpleasant. By now, every first drink of the day I had to have in easy accessibility of a lavatory: I had been blessed with daily diarrhoea! It was related to jangling nerves and always started as I took the opening 'shots' and first cigarettes of the day. Needless to say, this meant I had to give serious thought to where and when I took this daily combination of 'little comforters'! For example, I could no longer drink in a bar for fear of the loo being occupied, and usually not in someone's home for similar reasons. I would always make sure I had a few big ones before arriving on scenes such as these. Fortunately I used only to have one attack, so the rest of the day and evening passed quite comfortably from this point of view!

Mentally I had also started to anguish over the financial costs of my way of life. By now I virtually chain-smoked from the moment I took the first drink of the day. This meant my daily expenditure was two packets of twenty cigarettes, four or five bottles of wine, taxis to and from wine bars, prostitutes, and any other miscellaneous expenses (like food: though mostly I could not eat!) along the way. So the financial cost of my addictions was starting to hurt, though I admit this was the least of the worries that now consumed me.

Almost equally *embarrassing* was when I then had to put my business, *Training Dynamics Ltd,* into receivership. This was because I was inebriated by early afternoon almost every day. As I was not starting work until mid-morning due to hangovers and my drinking started at lunchtime, not much work was getting done at all! Creating the business a few years earlier had given me a great boost to my pride, but telling my family and friends of its collapse was excruciatingly painful and another massive blow to my *pride*. Needless to say there was much *dishonesty* surrounding my description of its downfall!

Fortunately for me, as a result of my rather dubious property and stock market ventures, I had about £40,000 left in the bank. I figured out that at my current rate of spending of approximately £10,000 a year I had enough to last me nearly five years. By then I would be almost 45 years old, and at the speed I was going, definitely dead!

Training Dynamics Ltd (TDL) had evolved out of an American training consultancy I was managing in Europe called *Thomas Blodgett Associates* (TBA). I had worked for *Xerox Corporation* for several years before this, selling their sales and management training programmes to large European multi-national companies. Tom Blodgett, their ex chief executive, heard about me and offered me the job of opening a London office for his up and coming New York-based consultancy firm in the same line of business. I jumped at the opportunity and left Xerox immediately. As I saw it, this was a highly dignified profession and a prestigious position; I could actually call myself 'a Management Consultant', which I thought of as just right for my image! I had first come across 'Management Consultants' in the mid- sixties when I worked in Northern Ireland and had been most impressed with this as a job title - I hoped then that one day I could aspire to such dizzy heights, but never imagined I would.

Dignified professions and active chronic alcoholism are not good bedfellows! Tom used to have me regularly attend business meetings at his New York offices. These took place on East 73rd Street in Manhattan. On my second or third visit I discovered the notorious '*Maxwell's Plum!*' This was a large, busy 'singles' bar only a few blocks away and ideal for a young man about town, in fact for me it was the perfect pick-up joint and New York's equivalent to my watering-holes back in London. I felt absolutely at home as soon as I walked in.

On one my visits I had a wealthy friend from the Middle East, whom I knew from my partying days in London, staying in New York too. He was the top arms dealer from Kuwait and had buckets of money to spend. I met him at *P.J. Mellons,* close by, where we had several large, Manhattan-style cocktails. We landed at *Maxwell's Plum* an hour or so later where we quickly met two pretty girls from Texas with accents and assets to dream about. We plied them with champagne until such time as they wanted to eat, which by then was the last thing on my mind. As a result they drifted off and we sought more amenable company elsewhere in the bar. We continued to talk to any pretty girls who cared to listen and eventually, after several more bottles of champagne, got very drunk. By 2 a.m. the bar was virtually empty except for a few other failed stragglers like us. My friend sensibly decided he had had enough and got a taxi to his hotel. As Tom was frugal on expenses, I had a bed on the floor of the office, and somehow I found my way back there. My homing device always worked no matter how drunk I seemed to get, something I have never been able to understand as I was always in blackout at such time. I then continued drinking until I passed out.

The next thing I remember it was early morning. I came to, lying on the office toilet floor. It was so small and I had to lie in the knees-tucked-up-to-my-chin position. I carried on sleeping there in between bouts of vomiting and diarrhoea for several hours. I had never felt more ill in my life. I was still there at 11 a.m. when I heard voices coming up the stairs. I had completely forgotten that we were due to have a business meeting that Sunday morning!

There was nothing I could do about it. I just lay there sleeping and heaving for another few hours. At last, I started to sober up. After washing in cold water, I hesitatingly made it to the office where the meeting was taking place; the one that was meant to have been my bedroom! I walked in, said not a word and sat down. I noted the awful mess I had left the room in. There were a few glances but no one spoke to me either. I must have looked absolutely terrible. Gradually the fuzziness disappeared and I was able to sip some water. Eventually I was able to mildly participate and thanks to the good grace of my colleagues, the subject of my condition was never discussed.

In the next two years I successfully implemented TBA training programmes for various multinational clients. During this time I realised I could 'borrow' the Xerox/TBA formula just as Tom had done, and do the same thing in a company owned by me. This way I would reap greater personal financial rewards and be on the road to a fortune. I did not take into account the effects alcoholism would have on this formula!

When sober during the daytime hours I was quite good at my job and I succeeded in running TDL alongside TBA without any serious hiccup for nearly a year. On one occasion I even astonished myself at my management capabilities. I had come into the office late morning still with the father of all hangovers. Almost instantly I had to make a series of major decisions to sort out a serious problem that had arisen with one of our more lucrative contracts. My staff were at 'sixes and sevens' and convinced we had got into an irretrievable mess and were heading for a calamitous fall.

My brain spun into action. I had never thought more quickly in my life. I made several direction - changing telephone calls, which resulted in everything being sorted out within half an hour. This was as much to my amazement as everyone else's and gave me back a stopgap credibility rating that in recent weeks had plummeted to near zero. If they had known of my mental state at the time they would have been even more impressed - I certainly was, and left almost immediately to celebrate. For a few hours I thought I could do anything!

It would be an understatement to say that 'chaos', based on my all too obvious *dishonesty,* then descended on both firms, like the black clouds did over Lagos several months later. (But that is another story!)

A practising alcoholic trying to run two identical businesses but with different names in parallel does not bear thinking about, let alone when he is trying to hide the existence of the one from the other set of employees. In my insanity I even had the TBA staff and my staff working in the same office! So some of my employees knew exactly what I was doing whilst the others became deeply suspicious. The whole ridiculous scenario caused serious undercurrents of tension for all concerned throughout most working days. My attitude to this was to bury my head in the sand and have another drink, hoping it would all go away and leave me alone.

It did not. In a very short time I had to get myself out of a huge mess; unfortunately this meant badly letting down people whom I really liked. What amazes me today is that *somehow I managed to blame Tom's 'greed' for what I had created!*

It is a fact that alcoholics never see themselves as the problem, it is always 'someone' or 'something' else's fault!

I now see my behaviour was also an example of another of the horrendous side effects of alcoholism and drug addiction: thrashing through the lives of other people, with little or no regard for their well-being.

A problem, therefore, with this seemingly uncontrollable behaviour was that in lucid moments I suffered terrible remorse over what my alcoholism was causing. The views of my conscience served to make me drink more to drown the unpleasant feelings of guilt that my behaviour entrained. And of course drinking more exacerbated all my other problems and brought with it even more guilt. It was all one massive vicious circle with its series of mind-crippling, knock-on effects.

As this way of life was now with me twenty-four hours a day, seven days a week, fifty-two weeks of the year without a break, it was no wonder that clouds had continued to darken my view of all aspects of my life. In a nutshell, I hated everything about life, about you – even if I had never met you - and me.

The descent of TDL into receivership took place with us working out of one room in my ever more disgusting Wigmore Street flat. By then I had accumulated three secretaries, an assistant, a manager and several consultants working for me. To add to the mayhem, as I was not *compos mentis* until mid-morning, almost all of the work was now done by them. (It would have been interesting to read my 'mission statement' had such things existed at the time. Something like: "With dishonest endeavours and as little work as possible, I try to satisfy all of our customers all of the time!" Perhaps?)

Much to my surprise, not all of the consulting work I did even now was a total disaster. One job with *Ciba Geigy*, the Swiss pharmaceutical giant, took me to Lagos, Nigeria for a week. This turned out to be the most interesting place I had ever visited, but that was not how I saw it at the time! From the moment I arrived my nerves were on edge. I had never been south of the Sahara before and the stories I had heard about violence and crime in Lagos meant I doubled my normal intake of Valium well before I landed. The payment of 'dash'- bribery money - had been explained to me at the same time as stories about bodies regularly washed up on beaches!

The first day there I ventured from the top-rated Eco hotel on Victoria Island where I was staying to the beach. It was a Sunday afternoon, very hot and humid. I had walked about half a kilometre when in front of me appeared the most extraordinary sea I had ever seen. Never before had I witnessed waves that had such incredible force. They pounded the beach with a might and consistency quite incredible to behold. I stood transfixed for several minutes taking it in, marvelling at the wonder of it all.

From where the beach started to the shoreline was quite steep and because of this I had not been aware of its closeness until I was virtually upon it. The Southern Atlantic waves that bombarded it with the consistency of a metronome were literally enormous. The sound was awesome and the whole effect I found spellbinding. I had my swimming costume with me and was a reasonably good swimmer, but there was no way I was venturing into that sea! Tiny children from about eight years of age swam without heed to the forces of nature that seemed to be buffeting them in all directions. I sat down and gazed at it for several hours, absorbing the scene. Even my fears left me as I enjoyed the spectacle of these tiny black children bobbing up and down with no regard whatsoever for their safety. I think what astonished me most was that it was obvious they were used to it and that for them this was just another normal Sunday afternoon on the beach. Best of all, for the first time in a long time, I felt good about life and that the real me had resurfaced. This thought did not last long!

That night, back at the hotel after dinner, I went to the disco. I had downed a bottle of wine, several local beers and became high in, and on, spirits. Again I could not believe what I witnessed. The large, dark room was full of young black women of most shapes and sizes. After a long searching look, I saw one who was by any standards sexy, aloof and very attractive. I quickly worked out a regime for myself. I knew I would get drunk each night, but I also knew the seminar I was administering was important: my future earnings very much depended upon its success. Each night, therefore, after a day's work, I would go to the disco, get absolutely blitzed and be in bed, very much alone, by midnight. On the last night I would make my play! The run-up worked a treat: but you may recall from Chapter 5 how, when I played my ace, the lady trumped me: my attempts to 'play it cool' backfired yet again! Somebody has since told me, *"If you want to make God laugh, tell Him your plans!"*

My other most memorable experience in Lagos happened on the penultimate day. It was about 6pm and I had just finished taking the fourth day's seminar. My driver had just started back towards the hotel. Within fifteen minutes everything had gone almost night-time dark. First, huge black clouds had formed and engulfed everything. Then, as if at some hidden signal, the heavens opened and rain fell as if poured from the sky in bucketfuls. Within minutes all the roads were about 15 centimetres deep with brown rivers running seemingly in every direction. Remarkably to me, my driver stayed unfazed and just kept driving. The people on the streets waded through the water as if it were not there, whilst I was almost speechless. Then the rain stopped almost as quickly as it had started.

After a few minutes I said, "This is incredible! I

have never seen anything like it in my life." The

driver said, "Oh it's nothing. It happens all the

time."

Again I marvelled at one of Lagos's natural phenomena, and equally at the way that the locals nonchalantly regarded it.

So within a week dark clouds had descended for me both externally and internally. As a result I will never forget my stay in Lagos. Though there was not quite enough material to write a whole book about it, I wonder what would have happened if I had spent a whole year?

From here I went to stay with a male friend and visit a girlfriend in Nairobi, Kenya. I was still very ill from my exploits in Lagos, and spent much of my six days there in a comatose state. I certainly did not impress those whom I had come to see, especially my girlfriend, who had been used to an outgoing, stimulating, fun-loving boyfriend a few weeks earlier back in London – how things change when alcoholism takes over a life!

Her name was Daniella, known lovingly to her friends as 'Dany'. We had been dating for several months and before Kenya, had got on really well in an easy-going kind of way. She was ex- Benenden Girl's School and an acquaintance of Princess Anne's. Her surname was Benting as in 'Benting's', the well-known insurance family name. Sadly, my abysmal performance in Kenya meant that our relationship came to a quick halt almost immediately she arrived back in England. So far Africa had really been working out well for me!

From Kenya I had arranged to visit a potential new girlfriend in South Africa. Her name was Sandra, and for several years we had been on the same party circuit in London before she had moved to Johannesburg. We would probably have got together sooner had it not been for my dating Maria at that time, as there had always been plenty of the right chemistry between us.

Before arriving, I had known little about apartheid and was quite shocked at the effect it was to have upon me. I took a taxi from the airport and on the drive in we passed through some very poor areas, some of whose history was described to me by my driver. From these very first encounters I found every aspect of apartheid appalling and failed to understand how such a system could have ever have come into existence in a once British Commonwealth country. But during my stay I kept these thoughts to myself.

This later identified for me yet another well-known character disorder of alcoholics and drug addicts: always being afraid to stand up for myself and to expose the real me unless I had a head full of alcohol or drugs to boost my confidence. The trouble with that approach was that it usually came out in the form of ever increasing resentment until I could stand it no more, and succumbed to emitting a stream of written or verbal abuse! The former is a slightly obscure example of 'People Pleasing', a well-known trait of many of us with addiction problems – we want to be liked but know that our behaviour is causing the exact opposite.

Sandra arranged for me to stay at the Balalaika Hotel in Sandton, an all-white area and the exact opposite to the shantytowns I had driven through on my way into the city centre. The hotel was a young person's paradise. On Friday nights it was vibrant with young people drinking and out for a good time – just like me! It was a Friday night. Almost immediately my Lagos blues were swept behind me. My friend had chosen well.

She arrived within about half an hour of my soaking up several drinks and the atmosphere; by then I felt very much at home. She looked terrific and was beaming with pleasure when she walked into the bar. She had made sure she had a clear diary for my stay and made it plain she was as delighted to see me as I was to see her. Over the next few days we had a very good time going to drinks, dinner parties and brais – the South African word for barbecues.

On one occasion, whilst driving past a cinema, she explained to me a lot about apartheid. I quickly started to loathe everything she told me. I could not believe that white people just like me could treat other members of the human race the way she described. She explained how there were cinemas and restaurants for whites or blacks only, where never the two were allowed to mix. It immediately reminded me of what I had witnessed in Northern Ireland between Catholics and Protestants, which I had found equally unpalatable once I had understood it. (In the years that lay ahead I was to become a huge Nelson Mandela fan and I still marvel at his incredible courage and temperament, both qualities I had dearly lacked all my life). The rest of my stay in South Africa went smoothly enough, but I never forgot the impact my encounter with apartheid had, helping me to develop a character of which today I am proud. Within two weeks of coming home my hopes for a love affair 'on the side' with Sandra took a massive turnaround.

Things with 'Dany' ended, not unexpectedly, within days of my landing – there is after all only so much from a perpetual drunk that anyone can take, especially as my attentions had become quite half-hearted – alcohol now came first in every relationship I had!

Instantly I was on the phone to Sandra suggesting another visit in the near future. I got an even more half-hearted response by letter in return. I will never forget its opening line:

Dear Jack,

As much as I enjoyed our time together last week, I am sorry to have to tell you that an old boyfriend has resurfaced and we have started seeing each other again. As we met before you came along it is only right I continue with him and see where it leads...etc.

Yours affectionately,

Sandra.

I did not bother to read past the first paragraph. I knew what it would say. More Valium and alcohol was my answer to anything resembling pain.

Meanwhile, back on the work front at TBA, conflicts had started to arise. Tom was ex-Harvard, Oxford and Cambridge, and I immediately thought, 'Great! I can say I am employed by a real Ivy Leaguer!' In addition to his academic credentials and Park Avenue background, I had grown to like him and hated my *dishonesty* with regard to what I was doing to our relationship. On my visits to his offices in New York I had met his family too, and other than finding him mean money-wise I can honestly say he was as fair as anyone for whom I had ever worked. He definitely did not deserve to be treated badly.

But my *greed* was out of control, and a total separation eventually took place. As a result *Training Dynamics Ltd* came into being and I thought my road to financial paradise lay just around the corner!

Unfortunately, I did not realise that a virtual one-man business needed the 'one man' to be present and working most of the time! My hours were, to say the least, erratic! I would arrive at my office between 9-30 a.m. and 1 p.m, accompanied by a most horrendous hangover and with little intention of doing anything other than the simplest tasks. I tried to delegate everything. I employed Barbara, Delia and Helen as secretaries, with Lawrence as training consultant, who between them did the bulk of the everyday work. Also, there were several part-time, self- employed management consultants who worked on projects as they were needed. God knows what they all must have thought I was doing, but none of them ever asked as far as I can remember.

For a time we survived on previous contracts where I had

been paid reasonably well and from which a little money was still coming in. I think I must have been fairly generous with their salaries as there were no complaints. As they did almost all the work, this was more to do with my fear of going out of business if I lost them, than any sliver of human decency on my part – at the time *I never did anything for anyone unless there was something in it for me!* Gradually, of course, we ate away at the pot until, in the end, the bank called me in for a reckoning. I had no answers and no assets; also I knew I had no prospects!

TDL therefore quickly died a sad death and was put into receivership: another huge blow to my *pride,* especially as I knew that if I could have got my act together it could have been a highly successful business. As it was I was back on the dole; this time enforced and with no likelihood whatsoever of my ever working again! I was 37 years old and the road ahead looked long, miserable, and very, very wide!

*Today, I remember clearly how I told lies upon lies upon lies to my family and friends to cover up my demise, as by now I knew it was my drinking and drug-taking that was the cause of **all** my problems. And it was that which I was too ashamed to tell anyone.*

***

Even shopping under hung-over conditions can be hazardous! By the time I was 38 almost all my wardrobe was purchased from charity shops. My shoes, socks and underpants were still bought new, but everything else was second-hand. I even knew which were the best Oxfam outlets to find designer labels!

Some cast-offs were fantastic value, especially on Marylebone High Street. On one occasion I bought a silk and velvet, red and black smoking jacket made by Turnbull and Asser of Jermyn Street for £24-00. I remember thinking how it would give me *style*! I gave no thought as to when I would wear it, and it certainly was not a 'must have' for my current life-style! In fact, other than trying it on when I got home, the only time it was ever worn was when a friend borrowed it one Saturday night for a fancy dress party. To make my lack of need for it blatantly obvious, my unfortunate friend had to report next day that in his stupor, it had been stolen! I never missed it, even for a second!

Another 'great' purchase I thought I had made was of a pair of moon boots from Marks and Spencer for £4-00. This was wayward thinking of the extreme kind! Firstly you do not need moon boots when you live off Oxford Street, Central London. Also they were marked down because they were 'odd' – two left feet, *and* they were at least one size too big!

The best example I had of reckless, blurred vision buying had been at Harrods a few years earlier. Wearing my usual chronic hangover like a shroud over my dulled mind, I had made it to opening time on the first day of the winter sale. I had just acquired a flat on Putney Hill, which had been decorated and now needed furnishing. I was flush with money from my dubious share dealings and was out to buy furniture to impress any girls who cared to enter my fairly luxurious bachelor pad.

My first port of call was to the fourth floor. I grabbed an assistant whom I briefed as to my requirements. Within minutes I had settled for a suite of dark brown matching teak and leather furniture, comprising an armchair, a huge three-piece loose sofa and an extra-large square coffee table. To this I added the most hideous pink suede armchair imaginable; a mahogany dining table and set of chairs; two double beds and other similarly unnecessary and incidental undesirables.

Lastly I went to the carpet department. I already knew exactly what I wanted. Recently, in a Sunday colour magazine, I had seen an advertisement where a most sumptuous naked girl lay on the thickest, white pile, woollen carpet in such a way that I thought to buy it would guarantee me wonderful sex for ever more in exquisite surroundings – nothing could have been further from the truth! But Harrods had exactly what I was looking for and I optimistically placed the order.

A few hours later, having squandered thousands of pounds on my attempts to find happiness in materialism, I set off for the 'Bunch of Grapes' on Brompton Road to celebrate my future conquests. I was 100% convinced I at last had a winning hand, certain to get me the most desirable girls in London. It did not and the carpet was only ever used for walking on!

Within weeks it was all installed and I moved in. The trouble was my head and habits did too!

The very first night I fell asleep in the armchair with a cigarette burning in my hand. Next morning when I awoke, as well as an empty bottle of whiskey, there was a horrible three-inch burn on the £750 coffee table where the cigarette had fallen! Needless to say this was only a forerunner of things to come, and much of the three years I spent living there I stayed just as unhappy as I had ever been.

It took me many more years to get the message that shackling myself to materialism and beautiful women would never give what I, as a human being, needed to be truly happy in this life. But that is another story and I needed a lot more adventures in alcoholism and drug addiction before I reached that point of self-knowledge!

***

Bed-wetting also became a prominent feature. The first time it occurred, I wondered, 'What the hell has happened?' But as my narcotic-induced, stupor-ridden years rolled by it was to become yet another horrible norm for me. In fact I was to do it so often that my mattress eventually had the pungent stink of stale urine from several feet away: something you may guess I was not too proud of!

Many mornings, ever hopeful of getting a girl back that night, I would lie the mattress down on its side and try to dry it out with a hair dryer. I would do this regularly, but whatever I did the smell would still be there. I even tried spraying it with anti-fungus and perfumed air sprays, but nothing worked; and anyway, I always did it again that night or a night or two later! So I wrapped it as tightly as possible in as many sheets as I could find to try to keep the smell hidden.

Fortunately I can only remember it actually happening on one occasion with a girlfriend. She had just woken up and said, "Jack, the bed's wet, what's happened?"

I did not dare say a word. I lay there motionless, pretending to be asleep, knowing only too well the cause. Shortly after, she got up and went to the bathroom followed by the kitchen. Sheepishly I did the same, letting a good many minutes go by first, as I suspected she would have guessed, but hopefully would be too polite to say anything further. She did not, but that did not stop more shame adding to the depths of self-disgust with which I was now living permanently.

I found many other physical aspects of alcoholism hideous, but 'the shakes' was one of the most embarrassing. The first time anyone saw me in this state was at Campden Hill Tennis Club in West London. It was one of the oldest, most prestigious tennis clubs in England. I had been a member there for many years, but by now I had a reputation as a heavy drinker and womaniser. It was a Saturday morning and I was having coffee with Natalie, a good and valued friend of long standing . I had just sat down and reached out to pick up my cup.

She said, "My God, Jack, look at your hand!"

I looked at it and could not believe what I saw. I had never seen it like this. It literally quivered, and there was absolutely nothing I could do about it. My face flushed badly and I made some pathetic excuse about 'a heavy night with the boys', and tried to change the subject.

Inside, though, I was terrified. Natalie knew what it was all right and said so. This was the final proof, too, of what I had already started to acknowledge – whatever lies I might like to tell myself: I was a chronic alcoholic! And Natalie being Natalie, I realised it would be around the club in no time. So for the second time in a matter of weeks I was aware my number was up!

From then on my shakes got worse. In the end, to take the first drink of the day, I had to do it on my knees. It had become impossible to hold a glass to my mouth and drink in the usual way as my hand literally shook too much and totally uncontrollably. To combat this I would fill the glass to the brim with cheap white wine; then on my knees, I would put my head down and drink as much as I could by lapping and sucking. This way I could take in just enough to calm my jitters. I would then, with the shakes having lessened, drink the rest in the usual way. About halfway into a pint of wine I would have enough inside me for the shakes to cease; I would then lose my fear of being seen and could return to what I thought was normal drinking! Did I say 'Normal'?

In a nutshell, I was out of work and my drinking and drug-taking were out of control. *My alcohol intake ranged from three to five bottles of wine daily, as well as much beer and spirits on top. Added to this, I took between 150 and 300 milligrams of tranquilizers - Valium and/or Ativan - a day, and between three and five sleeping pills - Mogodon or Euhypnos forte - every night. The total amount of alcohol and drugs was approximately the same each day. Added to this I experimented with cannabis and anti-depressants whilst smoking between 30 and 60 cigarettes daily. I started the latter when I was aged 15.*

Looking back today aged 62, I marvel at the fact that I am still alive and have been abstemious of all these substances for over 22 years. I had built up my tolerance to these levels gradually over 25 years of daily abuse, and understand from the medical profession that if a normal human being were to take these quantities of drugs in a day, on a one-off basis, he or she would be totally knocked out – and probably forever!

As a result of my experience I have been asked my views as to the ease with which alcohol and prescription drugs are available to the public. I have concluded it is best for me if I keep off this subject; just remembering that for me they are poisons, and each one, if I take it, will be a threat to my life. And that is all I need to know.

***

By now I shared my sumptuous flat at Bryanston Court with two 'middle class' friends, Annabelle and Angus. Both were a good few years younger than me, and because of what I had by then achieved, they seemed to view me as some sort of success – I certainly did not! Annabelle was very much the 'English rose' type and perfect for the image I had spent years trying to create; Angus was a chartered account with one of the world's leading accountancy firms and had a similar lifestyle to mine. We all shared hedonistic tenancies and in the evenings often had lots of fun together as well as with other friends.

I was out of work, and most of the day absolutely bored with life. Usually, around lunchtime, I started drinking. Annabelle and Angus were both at work and, I hoped, did not know the state my alcohol consumption levels had reached. I tried to hide this from them by filling a pewter pint tankard with vodka, wine and beer, and top it up with blackcurrant juice. The mixture frothed nicely, and with a purplish, pink tint on top, achieved my aim of looking 'different'! In fact it looked quite odd and tasted unusual too, but by now I did not care what I drank as long as it was alcohol.

I have since discovered that alcoholics will go to extreme lengths to hide their drinking: I therefore was no exception!

I happily consumed several of these large 'cocktails' daily until my friends came home. Annabelle would arrive first. I would try to pretend my drink was soft and fizzy but I am sure it did not fool her, as I would be three parts cut by then and behaving accordingly. Over the previous few years she had witnessed at first hand the downward spiral of my alcoholism, and I suspect she would have known even if I were only thinking of taking a drink! Angus would arrive a little later and he and I would set about drinking beer as if London's supplies were going to run out the next day. After a few pints we would go to a pub, returning around closing time. On the way home we would buy cans of beer or bottles of wine from the off-licence and back at home play *'Blondie'* until I passed out. (What I now find extraordinary is that if I was at home alone and in the same state, I would listen to Wagner, whom I adored as long as there were no vocals to get in the way of his woefully melancholic music. Maybe I actually had some latent intellectual tastes after all, I wondered?)

To satisfy my newly discovered artistic taste I found an artistically inclined girlfriend. Her name was Alice. I had known her several years and had always fancied her like mad, but until now she had always had a boyfriend. She was an amateur artist and exhibited her paintings on Bayswater Road every Sunday. I thought that with her good looks, love of tennis and skiing, kindly demeanour and contemporary lifestyle, she was the perfect girl for me. I actually thought we might live happily ever after. The trouble was, she was set in her ways and so was I!

Even though I was not working, easily the worst day of the week for me was Sunday – I hated its 'empty' feeling. With this in mind, I considered Alice was going to be good for me by filling both my Sunday and artistically devoid gaps. I quickly discovered my assumptions about these were not that good either!

Almost every Sunday at around midday for about nine months I would set off to meet her on my bike – it was the seventh year after my second ban of drink driving and when I was sober I travelled everywhere on it. Alice had several artist friends who had 'pitches' next to hers with whom she used to drink at lunchtime: I was always invited to join them. The trouble was that I needed a lavatory to be immediately on hand to cope with my diarrhoea when I took the first drink. As there were not many loos in the middle of Bayswater Road, I was stumped!

To get around it I would only briefly join her and drink something soft. Immediately after, I would hightail it back to Bryanston Court where I could drink in peace until I met up with her again in the evening. She was always amazed as to how I could be so drunk when I had refused to accompany her and her companions just a few hours earlier! Even though I was longing to share my alcoholic agonies with someone, and Alice was fully aware of my drinking problem and would have had a sympathetic ear, I did not have the courage to tell her the depths my addiction had reached – *pride* and *fear* had me in their deadly grip. I thought, 'Only the most pathetic kind of man could sink this low', and I did not want to admit to that to her or anyone else! *Yet that, I later discovered, was the key to the solution of breaking my addictive habits – become broken and then 'surrendering to win'!*

Planning our evenings together also was a serious problem. *Everything* I did revolved around taking the first alcoholic drink and my immediate need for a lavatory. In the summer we would often go to the Proms at the Albert Hall. She would drink wine in the interval, which I knew I could not because I was not certain to find a loo cubicle before the 'runs' started. Also, if I drank then, I would need at least one and a half bottles of wine immediately just to keep me going until the next break. At the same time I chain-smoked the first ten or so cigarettes, and smoking was not allowed in the Albert Hall arena. To get by I would double up my intake of drugs and wait until we got home and then hit the booze big time. This did not impress Sheila who had to get up to work next morning.

Everywhere I went this drinking formula had to be followed, so it was far better for me if the first few drinks were taken when I was alone at home. *The trouble was I sometimes thought I could still handle booze and kept forgetting 'panic attacks' had become part of my life as well!*

For years I had played tennis at weekends at Campden Hill tennis club. But now things were very different and I hardly played at all. Optimistically, I would set off on my bike for the club, usually just after lunch. Timed this way I could get over last night's hangover and be somewhat sobered up. Unfortunately, as I neared the club I would become more and more petrified of meeting people and would badly need a drink. In the last few hundred yards I would become riddled with a totally irrational fear. I thought *they* would see my blood-vessel lined face, blood-shot eyes and shaking hands, then accuse me of being a dipsomaniac: a description that had always terrified me.

On numerous occasions, having cycled the four kilometres to the club, I would get within fifty or so meters of the entrance, turn around and go immediately back home to safety. As soon as I arrived there, I would go straight to the kitchen, grab a bottle of wine and dive into the loo. A form of relief followed, but not one that was doing more than a most scanty patch-up to my totally disintegrated self-confidence!

Other embarrassing moments along similar lines became commonplace. Early one afternoon I was standing in an off-license desperate for a drink - I was also desperate for the loo! I could hold it no longer and the wet, tacky trickle of pee descended down the inside of my leg! I was transfixed with shame; I did not dare move in case I lost control of the flow and my moving would reveal the pool of urine that by now encircled my feet. I handed the shopkeeper the money and once I was sure I had finished peeing, I walked out of the shop as nonchalantly as I possibly could. When I reached the door I broke into a gallop and was back in my flat in no time, bottle open, trousers down, diarrhoea flowing and realising I could never go back to my local off-licence again!

Similar incidents to this also happened in taxis and other public places on numerous occasions but none were quite as memorable as this one. But each one notched up further wounds to my mental demise and overall misery.

***

Just as everyone else seemed to have known for several years, *I was now ready to admit for the first time in my life:* **'I am an alcoholic'.** The trouble was, I also believed that I had nowhere left to turn and *that* was the scariest part of all. Little did I know that I was about to meet the woman of my dreams who was to have the *answer to all my problems,* and what was amazing also was that she did not know she had the answers either! I had reached the point when I would have given every penny I had, and my left and right arms, to buy my freedom from booze and drugs. Yet the solution was free of all financial costs and at the same time, would lead me to a life beyond anything I could ever have imagined. As the old saying goes: "When the pupil is ready, the teacher appears," and Boy! Was this pupil ready!

PART 2

"JOURNEY INTO LIGHT"

Chapter 7

THERE IS A WAY OUT

When, at the age of fifteen, I had been innocently sipping shandies with my father, I would not have believed it possible that a nice boy like me could end up on the brink of skid row just twenty five years later. Or that the adolescent who had devoured love-story comics in his mid-teens could have had such a chequered history with women and failed to find his own perfect love match. But in the latter years of my alcoholism I blamed those early shandies and the fact of not having found 'true love' for the terribly depressed state surrounding all my present circumstances.

As a result of my self-centred character defects I had either treated girlfriends totally selfishly or let them walk all over me. Each way I turned I used my relationships with girls for excuses to get drunk. Looking for 'Miss Perfect', I had got the rules all wrong and as a result I was never happy with anyone. But in my misguided way I always thought true love was waiting just around the corner, and when it was not, I drank even more.

To sum up, I was *never* satisfied with any girlfriend, always finding something wrong with each of them, even Ginny, my joint all-time favourite. Virginia had all the qualities I had ever dreamed of in one person, and what was more she liked me equally too. Her infectious, instant humour; honesty, sparkling intelligence, caring, down-to-earth personality, no make-up, casually dressed attitude made her terrific company - whilst her tall, slim figure and feminine, fresh-faced looks made her especially good to be seen with. Also she played the piano: and I quickly developed romantic notions of her serenading me nightly as we meandered lovingly into old age together. What more could I have asked for? With her by my side I was relaxed and the good times I was sure would flow. For several months they did.

Sadly she smoked, but that was all she did wrong! But it was enough to bring my controlling, wanting-everything-my-own-way tendencies gradually into play. This added to my pathetic neediness, eventually leading to my smothering our relationship to death. (As I smoked too, it now makes my attitude seem even crazier!)

She lived in North London whilst I was in my flat near Marble Arch. She was working; I was not. To get to work she needed to leave my place before 6 a.m., drive home, shower, change and dress for work; whilst I lay in bed most of the morning getting over my hangover and feeling sorry for myself. Totally self-centredly, never once did I consider the extra effort she had to put into dating me, which in the end she remarked upon several times: I ignored this attitude hoping it would just blow away!

All I could think of was my fear of dying. By now I was terrified of having a heart attack in my sleep and as a result tried hard to persuade her to stay with me every night. But she refused, pointing out that she had needs too. But I persisted and eventually drove her away! I was too afraid to tell her the truth, as I thought that if she knew she would think me a wimp and abandon me forever.

Several other girlfriends I fell for told me they were having affairs with other men at the same time they were sleeping with me. On hearing this horrendous news, I would get insanely jealous, using it as the perfect excuse for drinking into a rage: saying to myself, and anyone who cared to listen, *"If you had my girlfriend problems, you would drink too!"*

Every one of these nightly drunken sessions would be followed by oblivion and even more remorse the next day. It was now I realised for the first time that alcohol was the depressant I was always told it was. The trouble was, as with every other negative aspect of my life, I had had to find out the hard way. I just would not listen to those wiser than me, always thinking I knew best!

Many of my girlfriends came from rich or well-known families and had middle-class backgrounds: these I always thought were better than me. Others were not good enough because they did not come from rich or middle-class backgrounds! The ones I wanted I could not have, and the ones I did not want I could have – I just could not find a winning formula. The only common factor was that they were always good-looking as this was essential for my superior self-image. But usually, once we had made love, I would go off them as the need to satisfy my super-enlarged ego was over and the challenge fulfilled. My going off them I would rationalise by ridiculous mental reasoning: either their breasts were too large or too small, their legs too thick or too thin, they spoke with the wrong accent, were not intelligent enough, or they had 'slept around' and were 'easy lays' - and so it went on until I was totally dissatisfied and ended the affair. I never looked at their qualities as human beings or ever thought that it was my thinking that was wrong!

Sometimes, though, I let the relationship drag on, getting

more and more depressed, until in the end I despised the girl concerned and the situation I was in. This was usually when they were very rich, super-attractive, or several things about them were good for my image and I thought I was getting something more than just physical satisfaction.

About this time I realised I had never had sex, not even once in my life, when I had not been under the influence of drugs and/ or alcohol!

With those whom I did want but who did not want me I would become chokingly possessive and sooner or later get ditched. But sometimes with these I would cling on for dear life allowing myself to be badly mentally abused until in the end they or I could take it no more.

Whenever I looked back, which with so much time on my hands I often now did, I could see the saga of my romantic life had been made up of one sad failure after another – and 'they' were always the problem never me! Also, I knew deep inside that most of my relationships had been for the wrong reasons, and when they ended, had left both them and me in tears: followed in my case by even more depression and the ensuing despair that always went with it.

As I had grown up to believe that one of the main criteria for a successful life was to find the 'perfect' woman, I now believed that due to my current state of addiction I had no hope of ever finding true happiness. At the same time I thought there was no way of my ever quitting the booze and drugs: so on all fronts death was the only way out, and that I was hammering, not knocking, at its door. But I also knew I did not have the courage to take my own life, so I wallowed in self-pity, trapped in a vice of the stalest of stalemates!

Little did I know, though, that the looming series of events was about to change my life forever!

***

Suddenly, as if out of the blue, there she was: rich, single, attractive, and most of all, she almost instantly wanted to live with me and raise a family! I could not believe it. Where had this 'angel' come from, and why, I wondered later, did I have to meet her in a wine bar when I was completely paralytic?

I did not argue with her wishes and neither did my psychiatrist; though even he could not have known the effect meeting her was going to have on the rest of my life. Although it seemed utter madness at the time, even to me in my very hazy state, it turned out that getting married at 39 was the best thing I had ever done. Not only did a contact through my marriage eventually lead to saving me from my addictions; I now had someone who could tell me on a daily basis what I had done the night before: an illumination that had been sadly lacking for many years!

Unfortunately our relationship quickly hit rocky ground! Due to my below-the-radar-screen moral standards, I already had a part-time live in girlfriend: Jessica-Jane, an ex British West Indies air stewardess from Barbados via Jamaica. Breaking the news to her of my impending marriage did not go down well, but my lust for money came first and on I went with my marriage plans. But my 'new love' did not stop me on my last night of single freedom attempting a 'ménage a quatre' with her, her cousin and my best man! For the record it backfired badly like most of my other insane, drunken ideas: these good Christian ladies with high moral values, rightly, did not want to know!

Another of my ill-conceived, pre-marriage 'ideas' also went badly wrong!

Some years before my proposal of marriage being accepted, I had met Barbara Jones who lived and worked near my Wigmore Street flat. She had been christened 'The Face' because of her gorgeous and fresh good looks, after some modelling she had done the previous year. We met at a party and had flipped over one another instantly.

Our Thursday evening opening amorous rendezvous was as good as it gets. Drinks at her place followed by dinner at my favourite first date restaurant, La Paesana. She drove us there in her luxury new Triumph TR7. I had rung Toni in advance to make sure he pulled out all the stops: he did, extolling her with his Latino charm and paying compliments to me all evening.

Barbara looked radiant, seemed enamoured with me, and what's more, did not drink alcohol! To begin with this worried me but as I finished the second bottle of wine and ordered a third, she picked up the bottle and poured me a drink. As she filled the glass almost to the top she said the immortal words:

"I don't drink because of my figure, *BUT I love a man who does!*"

Here was my sort of woman all right, and the look in her eye confirmed it. We gaily talked for another hour and then as I ordered the forth bottle of wine, I had a brainwave!

I said, "I know we've only just met, *but I know you are made for me. Let's get married'*. It was the first time I had ever said these words, and even though she was an almost absolute stranger I thought I meant them from the bottom of my heart. What was more, she did not say no! I gently persisted with this line a little longer and then we went back to her place.

There was no hesitation about inviting me in, or any doubts in my mind as to the way this was going! Once inside her elegant, second floor flat off upmarket Marylebone High Street, she poured me one of the largest whiskies I had ever seen – it was like being in Heaven, this girl knew *exactly* what I needed! We sat on a well-cushioned sofa and immediately started petting. It was shortly after our first long embrace she said our third immortal phrase of the evening: this one though had a very different ring!

"I have a lover who's married and lives in Texas. He bought me the car, the flat and pays for almost everything. He comes over every few weeks and we always meet in the South of France. He's the boss of our law firm and doesn't want anyone to know about us. He usually only gives me a day or two's notice". There was hardly a pause for breath whilst I inhaled deeply!

All this she said quite matter-of-factly as if she was delivering the weather forecast: and in a way I suppose she was!

I had a monumental temperature rise, which had an instant sobering effect. I squirmed inwardly but kept my feelings to myself; I knew I would blow everything if I opened my mouth. I needed the whiskey and used it to the best effect:

then another. It worked and gave me the courage to pursue my more immediate lustful goal.

I thought, 'If she sleeps with me, I am sure she will ditch this hideous lover and we'll live happily ever after'. Needless to say she was only half on my wavelength!

We went to bed and soon all my immediate worries were forgotten. Next morning nothing was said about the lover and I was too afraid to mention my offer of marriage. I 'knew' we were very much 'in love' and that was all that mattered: time would sort everything out.

About 9 o'clock she made breakfast, one last lingering caress and off she set for work. I walked with her as it was on my way home and all we talked about was how we would spend the weekend together, doing the things lovers do. We cooed all the way to her office in Queen Anne Street, where we said our 'au revoirs': then I went, mentally skipping all the three blocks home!

Just before lunchtime she rang and uttered our forth immortal, line in 24 hours:

"Tom has just rung and wants me to be in Cannes tomorrow for two nights. I'm really sorry but I have to go. Can I see you Sunday night instead?"

I was devastated. I said, "but you can't after what we said and did last night *and* again this morning!'

She said "I have too". And she did.

That was the way my fling with Barbara went: weeks

enjoying the view from the highest mountain followed by days wallowing in the deepest, darkest valley. I had realized her schedule meant I would have much more time with her than without and thought I might be able to handle it, but after a short time, I could not: my jealousy consumed me and reluctantly we parted. Sadly she did not put up a fight.

But now, with my wedding day just a few weeks' away, memories of her beauty and the way we were flooded back to me. It was then I knew I could not get married until I was sure she was not the 'right' one after all!

I discovered she had moved to Houston and broken up her relationship. I rang and she was as keen to meet as I was. I was on almost the next plane; planning to stay at least a week. As soon as we met it was not the same – she had put on weight! She slept in her bedroom and I slept on the living room sofa. Too much water had flowed under the bridge for both of us and I recognized it instantly. She took me for a lovely weekend where we stayed with friends on a river estuary near Galveston in the Gulf of Mexico, but not even that could make it right again. All the time I was there I 'lived' on drugs and tried hard to muster up the same urges that I once had, but I could not.

I went back to London and married my dream woman.

*****

When I quit all mood-altering drugs nine months later, a new light shone on my cumulative activities over the preceding months as well. For example, my gorgeous wife, a St. John's Wood Jewish 'princess' in her early 30's, was able to remind me of a skiing holiday we went on with some of our friends to Switzerland earlier that year. I had no recollection of it whatsoever: not knowing where we had stayed, with whom we had been or that we had even gone - to begin with I did not even believe it had happened! As time went by I remembered the tiniest bits of it, but that was all, and that is the way it still is.

She also reminded me that our marriage had not started off too well! She told me how I had been hospitalised for drug addiction on our honeymoon in Jamaica.

My father-in-law, a most generous man, had provided us with a two and a half week holiday on this lovely island. I was almost broke and basically, he paid for everything, as he had done from the moment I met his daughter. Firstly we stayed with friends just outside Kingston before moving on to the luxurious Jamaica Inn. After a few days there, we went to the far end of the island to stay at Hedonism II, a resort notorious for living up to its name!

This was my kind of place, since smoking *ganja* was the 'in' thing. I hooked up with some doctors from New York who were going to a 'magic mushroom and *ganja* cake-eating party'. These were my kind of people. My wife was happy to come along too as I was not drinking, only taking drugs and they were an amusing crowd. All went well for the first few hours. The problem was, as always, once I started using I could never stop. I eventually ended up with horrendous hallucinations, thinking I was going insane or about to die, and being rushed to hospital. There I was pumped full of Valium and gradually calmed down. Now I knew what my wife meant about our marriage not starting off too well!

As I said though, getting married was the best thing I have

ever done. This was so in more ways than just to improve my memory. For weeks my wife had been telling me how her best friend had been off alcohol for several years. She suggested I meet up with her. I did so one Saturday afternoon at her Notting Hill home. I was fully 'loaded' and not in the mood to stop drinking. She suggested we meet again the following week and that she would take me to an AA meeting where she would introduce me to some friends who had also quit. This we did, and this time I met people who were just like me; people who had been hooked on alcohol, and many on drugs too: the difference was that they were all drug and alcohol free! I could not believe it; for years I had thought there was no one else like me on the planet.

It was suggested we meet again and go to another meeting, and this did a few days later. This time I was introduced to an Australian lady who had been sober - off alcohol and drugs - for a long time. She told me about a friend of hers who was the doctor specializing in alcoholism and drug addiction at the Charter Clinic in Hampstead, North London. She gave me his telephone number and suggested I ring him. That evening I did and he thought I should meet a counselor there called Bobby, to be assessed.

Next day I made an appointment to meet Bobby and saw her a few days after that. I turned up alcohol-free but full of tranquilizers – the great thing about 'tranx' is that they are legal and do not smell and so no one could tell when I had taken them. We talked for a long time and although I told her about my normal alcohol intake and its consequences, I did not mention the prescribed drugs.

For several years, on and off, I had often not drunk on

Sundays. Instead I would fill myself full of tranquilizers all day, and sleeping pills when I wanted to go to sleep at night. I kidded myself that I could not be an alcoholic if I did not drink every day of the week, fifty-two weeks of the year. As well as fooling myself, I *almost* fooled Bobby!

We had spent an hour discussing my arrests, blackouts, bed-wetting, shakes, diarrhea, hospitalisations and other pleasantries surrounding the less attractive aspects of my drinking. Suddenly she shrugged and said:

"Your drinking is certainly different. I have never met anyone who drinks as much and as often as you do but who can stop just like that." And with that she started concluding our meeting.

I stood up to leave and started to walk towards the door: suddenly, as if inspired, I turned and made the most world-changing statement that had ever passed my lips:

"Thank you again for your time," - I was still very polite - "it's easy. I just take more tranquilizers and sleeping-pills to see me through!"

I will never forget the show-stopping, earth-shattering impact of her next statement:

"Hold it right there! What do you mean, tranquilizers and sleeping pills?" she said as if she had found the answer to all the worlds' problems. In this case she had certainly uncovered the answer to all mine!

Bobby was well made, with a dynamic, forceful, well-meaning character, and as I looked back at her beaming face

I knew: *it was all over for me. I was found out at last!* I sat down again and this time I told her the whole story. I had never told anyone any of the true reality of my life before, and not even my wife knew about the 'tranx'. I was so ashamed of them: I had always thought it was only dear old ladies who took such things, not 'men': except, of course, pathetic me!

As a result of my once-in-a-lifetime's honesty, I was admitted for detoxification to the Charter Clinic on Sunday 28th July 1985. Retrospectively, I can see how the knock-on effect of meeting each of these marvelous people, starting with my wife, wondrously changed my life, and in the years that followed, my perception of what life is really all about.

On 12th August, two weeks later, a nurse administered my last ever mood-altering chemical; two milligrams of Valium. I have not had a drink, drug, or cigarette since. In the intervening years my life has changed dramatically. I no longer spend my days in fear of dying or of meeting friends with whom I have done something shameful. I am a respected, reasonably accomplished, equal- to-everyone, average citizen of the world - though I hope I will never forget I am an ex-drunk and junkie too! I have been given a role to play within my family, the work environment and in society. I run my own business, which gives me great pleasure and satisfaction. I am extremely grateful to be alive and I take life as it is dealt out to me, with all its ups and downs. Once again, I have friends, both old and many more new and, most importantly, I have learned how to be a friend too - and to love - myself.

As a result, I have discovered the true meaning of Love, which I now value more than any of the material gifts I have also been given. I came to realize in my early years of sobriety that I had always had all my values completely upside down and back to front. I have since come to believe that there is one loving God presiding over all that there is here on earth and in the universe. And then I discovered that He had always been looking after me, and today I know that He always will.

During my early years of abstinence from drink and drugs I took up interests again that I had long ago given up, but which I had loved in my childhood. I became interested again in the world of nature and the creation of our universe. In my spare time I studied astronomy, geography, geology, natural history, science, environmental issues, philosophy and the world's great religions. I found a depth and meaning to life that I had not known existed, and most surprisingly of all, I learned to pray and to meditate.

I gave up fiction's Iris Murdoch, Scott Fitzgerald, Tom Sharpe, Ed McBain and Dick Francis for the writings of Scott Peck, Emmett Fox, Deepak Chopra, Bill Wilson, Joel Goldsmith's *The Infinite Way,* Marianne Williamson and *A Course in Miracles:* and many other spiritually or philosophically inclined authors. I exchanged singles wine bars, pubs and nightclubs for AA and NA meetings, mosques, churches, temples, synagogues and Friends Meeting houses: I became a Quaker. My heroes became Mahatma Gandhi, The Dalai Lama, Nelson Mandela, Mother Theresa, Martin Luther King and Jacky Pullinger, replacing Humphrey Bogart, Richard Burton, Dylan Thomas, Barry John, Adam Faith and Philip Marlowe – though I still won't give up Raymond Chandler, watching *Casablanca,* or the 'BaBa's' beat the All Blacks every other year!

I got a job and went on holidays to places of interest instead of lazing half the day at the tennis club, in bars and on beaches. For fear, sloth, stupidity and hate I substituted courage, work and service, wisdom and love. I give money to charities instead of pouring it down my throat or losing it in casinos.

I discovered how to live in 'the spirit of the universe' and found that life at last had meaning. But most all I found freedom to be myself: though I have to add, there have been many self-created hiccups along the way!

But before all this I had to be detoxified, which needed close medical supervision. I was kept in the Charter detox unit for fifteen days with other patients coming and going all the time; mostly they stayed about five nights, the average for normal alcohol or drug withdrawal.

Alcohol was removed from me immediately. I quit cigarettes the same day too. A short, sharp tapering-off strategy was applied to the sleeping pills, and a slightly more gradual one to the tranquillizers. Most of the time I was terrified! I thought they were doing it all much too quickly. For the first three nights I hardly slept at all. The first night when I got out of bed to go to the bathroom my legs were like jelly and I literally wobbled onto the floor! I had never known an experience like it and thought I was going to be like this for the rest of life. As it transpired, each night got a little bit better.

On its own, alcohol withdrawal can be dangerous. Done at the same time as coming off tranquillisers, it was also terrifying; but by now I knew anything was better than drinking. I was put on anti-fit pills, *Epinutine*, to counteract the most dangerous side-effects – epileptic fits. But due to the quantities I was coming off and my recently developed tolerance to them, *Epinutine* did not stop me having such a convulsion. Fortunately another patient was with me when it happened, who immediately called the medical staff and I was put on an oxygen machine until I regained consciousness. I knew nothing about my fit, which added to my colossal fear as to my safety when it was explained that I might have others! Thankfully I did not, and after another six days I was told the danger period had passed. By then I had started hyperventilating.

When I had first been a patient at Regents Park Nursing Home in 1980, Max Glatt had warned me that sudden alcohol withdrawal was dangerous. He had prescribed the anti-fit drug *Epinutine* to prevent me having one. As by now I was trying to stop drinking, frequently using *Antabuse* and always failing, my fear of having such a fit helped me persuade my doctor and other psychiatrists to add *Epinutine* to my list of prescribed drugs. So by the time I got to Charter Clinic I was somewhat immune to the effect of anti-fit pills, hence my unexpected spasm whilst detoxing.

There is no doubt that my chronic fear of dying now helped save my life. Whilst I was at Charter I started to meet people who suggested I make changes to my way of life that would help me sort out some of the awful mess I was in. One of these was a doctor working there. I could not believe it when he told me how he had once had similar addictions to mine and how he had lived drug and alcohol-free for the past nine years! I thought it was incredible and impossible: a doctor telling me he had once been like me, and that he was today, in his words, "clean and sober". This was the first sign of hope I had known for years, and I will always remember his kindness in sharing his experience with me. Today he and I are good friends and I have deep gratitude for what his little talk did for me that day.

The other medical staff at the clinic were also incredible and I soon fell in love with all the female nurses - and some of the males as well! In many ways I felt as though I was loved back to life. I will never forget what they did for me, and my many withdrawal experiences there. I also had regular visits from both my psychiatrists, who found my cross addictions and amounts of drugs I had consumed so interesting that they thought of writing it up as a case study. Even though I was disappointed when they decided not to, I suspected this was only because they wished to protect me as much as possible from my ego, and in case I failed to make it!

In all the seven and a half weeks I stayed, about eighteen patients came and went – two of them committing suicide within days of leaving. This did not do a great deal for my already shredded confidence, but did provide me with enough fear to be determined to do my best to make sure their fate would not befall me: I was convinced I would be the next in line! One councillor kept reminding us that in her group of nine, she was the only one still alive and that all the others had died from addiction and alcoholism! Knowing my past history of falling at every hurdle it was no wonder I was worried!

After a few days I was told I had to attend 'group'. Mostly about eight of us had group therapy together every day where we were asked to talk about our experiences relating to alcohol and drug abuse. We were also urged to express our feelings about anything in our lives that caused us serious anxiety or resentment. It took me some time to catch on as to what they meant by "feelings" but once I got the hang of it I never looked back, and lots of anger surrounding my being an alcoholic and drug addict gradually came out. On one occasion it came out in such abundance that I started smashing up the furniture in the middle of a group session. As a result, and much to my surprise, I was then taken on one side by a counsellor and told I was doing well - I really had got a back to front attitude to life!

Similar expressions of honesty I later found out helped turn the key that slowly opened the door of my pathway to recovery. After a further six weeks of honestly sharing like this in 'group', it seemed as if I had been 'Humpty Dumptied', and had shattered into a million pieces. What worried me now was 'would the counselors be able to put me back together again?' They said without hesitation they would but it took a long time before I was convinced too.

Gradually my attitude and outlook to life changed. Patients who had attended the clinic in previous years visited us and shared their abstemious living experiences. This gave me a little hope, which was something I had been lacking for many years. Each one told their drink and/or drug-taking story and I always identified to some extent with each of them, whatever they had taken and whatever they had done.

I was later told that one of the key ingredients to recovery from alcoholism and drug addiction is for one alcoholic or drug addict to share their experience with another. I also found out it is the one doing the telling who is helped the most. I was also told I needed to be 'willing to go to any lengths' to stay sober, and I was.

One morning the dreaded pronouncement was made and I

was told I was ready to leave. I was afraid, but I now knew if ever I got into difficulties I had telephone numbers to call and people I could meet who would help any time of the day or night, who fully understood addiction and who were now living clean and sober lives themselves. It was also suggested I get a 'sponsor', someone who had 'been there too' and was now recovered. His job was to hold my hand and act as my 'guiding light' through the corridors of living, which would lead to a 'new found land', one beyond my wildest dreams: and it has.

When I first left Charter I rang at least three ex-addicts or alcoholics daily. I also went to daily AA and NA meetings where I found others who had been through the same wringer that I had, and who now lived normal, drug and alcohol-free lives. I was introduced to literature written by ex- drunks and drug addicts who had recovered and I started to read some of this daily as well. I found that all the structure was already in place for me to follow, tried and tested guidelines that would enable me to live a clean and sober life; all I had to do was follow the well-signposted directions. I did just that, I did not dare do otherwise. I clung to this new way of living as only the dying can do. I found some changes hard, but with my life at stake I had become willing to do anything to stay alive.

Needless to say, as well as not wanting to die, I had reached the point where I was prepared to try anything to get me out of the deepening gloom that had closed in on me, brought about by my twenty-five years of daily alcohol abuse and twenty years of drug-taking. Today, with hindsight, I see clearly the ever-spiraling downward effect those mood-altering chemicals had had upon me. Similar arrests in the United Kingdom and France, waking up on the floor of a police cell in North America; not knowing where I was, what I had done, or how I had got there, and my seedy experiences with prostitutes had been shattering experiences for someone as sensitive and 'delicate' as I. Such experiences, when added to my non-existent sense of self-worth, had gone from a gradual descent into freefall.

Chapter 8

MY SPIRITUAL DAWN

"Any fool can cut the grass,
It takes real skill to make it grow"

I had been free of alcohol and drugs for nearly three weeks. I was still in Charter Clinic and doing all I could to remain abstinent. Then one day at an AA meeting, an older man - who happened to be my sponsor's sponsor - with many years of sobriety behind him said;

"Every morning I get on my knees and pray to God for a 'clean and sober day'."

I thought to myself, 'he's wacko: I don't believe and never have believed in God!"

Then he added, as if he had been listening to my thoughts and as though he had said it ten thousand times before "We all start bemused, and then we learn '*to fake it to make it*'."

After a slight pause he said "At the end of the day I get on my knees and say 'Thank you, 'God' for keeping me clean and sober today".

It was then he played his ace of trumps, "And it's '*God, as you understand Him*'; even a light bulb if you want it to be. And for any newcomers I suggest you use the expression '*Higher Power*', it will be easier to get your head around."

He was right; even I had no problem with that.

After an even longer pause and a glance as if to see if I was paying attention, with the patience a loving father would have for his long lost son he said, "In my experience, 'living in the day' is the easiest way to view life without alcohol. More than that is too much for alcoholics like us."

Then to make it even easier, he suggested we get used to living life, '*Just for Today*' and '*One Day at a Time*'.

I have tried to do this ever since: though not always quite as efficiently as I would have liked!

A few days later, I was having trouble with the concept of 'God' keeping me sober. This time I met a long-time sober American who suggested I think of 'God' as though I were asking my real-life father for something, and once he had given me the 'gift', in this case sobriety, I was politely to say 'thank you': put like this I soon found praying easier to understand and God's 'gift' of a single clean and sober day a perfect formula to live by.

I had just finished being detoxified and was sharing a room with a cocaine addict. I had been totally drug-free for just over a week – I suddenly realized that this was the first time I had been without a mood-altering substance in my body for a single day in over twenty years! When I looked at it like this I could see how diabolical my situation had become and how it was not surprising my life had got into such a hell of a mess. As I was still absolutely petrified of drinking alcohol, that night for the first time in my life, I got on my knees and prayed from the bottom of my heart.

I said something like, "Please God, if You do exist, I beg You to help me with my drug and alcohol problem. I have tried hard for years to stop and failed every time. I am also terrified of dying. I promise from now on I will try to be good and lead the life I believe You would want me to follow." I then added, "Thank You 'God' for the clean and sober day I have just had. Amen."

That was it, and though nothing actually seemed to happen, there were no flashing lights or choirs of angels, somehow I felt good about what I had done. And most importantly of all, I was sober and narcotics free!

Next morning I was on my knees again: this time asking for help with my booze and drug problem for the next 24 hours, and as this action has worked with 100% success except for a handful of days in my early months when I forgot, I now see that with the help of these simple prayers, which take about thirty seconds each day, I am guaranteed to stay alcohol and drug-free 'just for that day'. As it has been like this for well over twenty years I doubt I will break the routine, especially knowing it is a habit that has better results than any of the horrendous habits I used to have!

Several weeks later, shortly after returning to my wife and home in St John's Wood, I started wondering more about whether there really was a God: and if so, how does one go about finding him?

I decided to try my local Church of England on Hamilton Terrace. There, on about my third or fourth visit, I sat behind two older ladies who, from the clothes they were wearing, belonged to the Salvation Army, or similar organisation.

After a while I leant forward and asked them, "I wonder if you can help me? How do I pray to God when I have little or no faith?"

I will never forget the reply given by the one directly in front of me. She turned around slowly, and looking over her left shoulder with the kindliest of 'I quite understand' smiles, quietly said with the Scottish brogue of Janet from 'Dr Finlay's Casebook':

"Well, what I say every morning is; *'God, I believe, help Thou mine unbelief. Please God, reveal Yourself to me and be real for me today.'*

With that, she looked at her companion, smiled broadly as though her mission was accomplished, and returned to silently and serenely facing the front of the church.

It was so simple I was quite taken aback. Yet I knew instinctively this was the answer and desperately sought to memorise what she had said: once I had it firmly ensconced in my mind I leaned forward and thanked them for the treasure they had just let fall into my life.

From that day forth I added these simple prayers to my 'clean and sober' request every morning. As time went by, at appropriate intervals, I was introduced to other prayers, each of which was perfect for the experience I was then going through; it was as if my journey had been carefully mapped out and all I had to do was follow the compass signs.

One other experience helped me as a beginner in prayer. It was when I heard this simple story. It summed up precisely where I was coming from.

A junior school teacher, Mr. Jones was taking a Religious Instruction class. Part of it was a description of prayer and how it is done by different religions. On his way home that evening, the path he took was through a wood. At one point he paused because he could hear someone talking. As he got nearer he saw someone sitting on a branch of a tree reciting the alphabet. When he reached it he stopped, looked up and realised it was one of his pupils from the lesson that day.

"Hello Johnny', he said, "why are you saying the alphabet over and over again?"

Johnny started to cry, then he replied very quietly, "I'm sorry Mr. Jones, I don't know how to pray. I thought that if I said the letters, God would put them into the right words."

Since those days I do not believe I have taken a single backward step, though many times it seemed I had gone several steps forwards only to encounter a huge slap in the face and end up going many back: so deeply rooted were the negative attitudes that haunted my stumbling progress. But a view of the 'big picture' today clearly demonstrates I had, at all times, been led along an ever-broadening, spiritually inclined path; even when I had been incarcerated at the bottom of life's pit! It was just that God and love were very well camouflaged whilst I was floundering in that self-constructed mire!

I also learned that a better self-worth had to be 'earned' in the same way that a spiritual life had to be 'practised' on a daily basis: there were no days off in my recovery from alcoholism! I found when I took positive action based on my moral beliefs I received esteem-building results: hence on a scale of nought to ten my self-worth has risen from zero to around seven or even eight on a good day. Conversely, when I took negative actions, I ended up thinking badly about myself and slid back down the scale again. In the same way I discovered the more I practised prayer, meditation and doing charitable things for others, the more my spiritual life grew and the less self- centred I became. This often meant my having to do things I did not want to do and not doing things I would like to have done: with the net result of my having a much more positive view upon life.

With me making good progress after completing the Twelve Step Recovery Programme of AA and NA, my wife became keen to have a family. On several recent visits to my doctor I was found to have a 'zero' sperm count, a side-effect of my alcohol and drug abuse. So there was great surprise when she became pregnant. As a result of this we decided to move to a five-bedroomed house in Hampstead, have a nanny and expand our family at a later date. Someone had told me that sobriety was *'a bridge to normal living',* but I certainly had not expected anything quite like this!

By now I was working as a stockbroker, which in itself had come about in a somewhat spiritually synchronistic way.

Due to my alcoholism I had not worked for several years: living on my £40,000 of savings from dubious share and property deals, plus social security. After six months of sobriety and much- needed rehabilitation both mental and physical, I had got a part-time voluntary job at London Zoo. Shortly after this I was offered full-time employment by a man in the carpet business.

He said at the interview, "And as well as everything else, you may have to clean the lavatories!"

I was horrified, but my sponsor reiterated my need for "any menial job you can get", so I took it. I had always hated getting my hands dirty and this was complete anathema to me. As it turned out, and much to my relief, I was never asked to scrub the dastardly loos. But I know I would have done it if I had been. My sponsor's words, *"You need to be willing to go to any lengths, Jack, if you intend to stay sober,"* reverberated through my brain: fortunately for me, I was.

After six months of fulltime employment I was told by friends that I should be capable of doing something more suited to my skills – I wondered what on earth they were referring to!

Around this time, my father-in-law, a successful entrepreneur, asked me what work I would like to do for the rest of my life, or would I like to work for him? He had retail and commercial property interests as well as wool and cashmere retail and manufacturing businesses. To the latter offer I quickly said no.

I had always wanted to be a stockbroker, but as I only had four 'O' levels and no public school background or university degree, I had always ruled that line of work out. These aspirations had come into being after a maths lesson when I was about 14 years old, when our teacher described stockbrokers and jobbers in a way that fascinated me. He also said they earned a lot of money for doing very little work, which fascinated me even more! His description had stuck with me all these years and as a result of my City contacts and nearly twenty years of share dealings, I said quite abruptly and much to my amazement,

"I've only ever wanted to be a stockbroker."

For the first time in my life I was being honest about my working ambitions. He immediately said he could 'fix it' as his partner's son was head of Hambros, Merchant bank, and 'Jimmy' Goldsmith's Number One takeover adviser. I instantly replied that I wanted to do it by myself, not for once imagining that I could actually make it happen. As it is I do not believe I did, but that Divine guidance took a hand in what happened next!

At a drinks party almost exactly a week later I met an older man who was quite drunk. In an arrogant way, he was quite friendly and after a while we got onto the subject of work. He said he was a stockbroker and we discussed the stock market and my experiences with takeovers for the next ten minutes.

Then he asked, "What do you do for a living?"

"I work for a carpet fitter," I replied, and out of the blue added, "However I'm thinking of becoming a stockbroker!"

I will never forget his answer or my surprise at my directness.

"Call my office on Monday morning and I will arrange for you to have an interview. We are looking for someone like you right now," he said with an assured authority.

We spoke quite a lot more with him telling me that his firm was called Fox Milton and that they were based near St Paul's underground station. As he was getting more and more tipsy, the rest, partly due to his incoherence and my head being in the clouds, I do not recall.

I could not believe my luck, but at 9-10 Monday morning I was on the phone to his office.

It was mid 1986, the booming, pre-crash yuppie market, and I was immediately offered a full-time position as a private client stockbroker. I resigned my carpet-laying job and started a few days later. Unfortunately, I realised almost instantly that they ran a highly dubious business!

They would buy blocks of what were tagged as 'penny shares', telephone their private clients and tell them to 'buy', suggesting that a take-over was imminent when it was not. The stock would be bought at say two pence and sold on to their clients at a slightly higher price, with commission added on top! It was scandalous and I knew I had to get out of there as quickly as possible. By now my moral values had returned and I was trying to live up to them.

As I was still very unsure of myself I telephoned a senior stock-broking friend in New York and told him what had happened. He had been sympathetic to my drink problem, and when he had lived in London a few months earlier, had helped direct me towards Charter Clinic. Now, though, he was a senior executive in one of America's biggest stock-broking firms.

He said, "You have to leave there immediately. Call the Managing Director of our London office and go and talk to him."

I did so and did not go back to Fox Milton. I had already

taken my things with me the night before, anticipating something like this. It was now Friday, and three days later I was in his London MD's office telling him my story. Our meeting turned into an interview and I was offered a job on the spot. I have never looked back work-wise, doing something I have enjoyed doing ever since.

Less than a week later I was working at Jeffrey's and Company, International Stockbrokers, Finsbury Circus, London EC2 – in The City at last! The day started for me at 7.30 a.m. Every morning I would walk across Hampstead Heath to the underground station almost skipping, I was so happy. I had always dreamed of carrying the 'FT' in one hand, briefcase and brolly in the other and catching the 'tube' in the rush hour, morning and night. As far as I was concerned, I thought I was at last doing the work for which I had always been destined.

A little over a year earlier, when I had been newly 'dried out', a long-time sober friend had suggested I write on a piece of paper two things I would like to have happen in the next twelve months. Then he said I should put it aside and look at it in a year's time.

I wrote down: 1. Work at London Zoo,
                 2. Become a stockbroker.

I could not believe it when I remembered this piece of paper and realised what had happened. I have marvelled at the workings of Providence and my good fortune ever since.

It had also been suggested that I write a 'gratitude list'. What on earth was that, I wondered?

"Starting with your sobriety, you write down all the things you have today for which you are grateful," my sponsor said. "It will always help you feel good about life and yourself," he continued, finally adding: "This has always been my experience."

That night I wrote my first ever 'gratitude' or 'blessings list', and he was right, it did help me to think positively and give me grateful-to-be-alive feelings – *"grateful alcoholics do not drink"* I have been told. Since then I have written many more and today I keep an on-going list with me at all times, which I add to every day. Still number one on it is that I am drug and alcohol-free. This by far is still the most important aspect of my life; for I know that without this, I would not have a life! My days of sobriety are followed by my family, many friends, the much travelling I have done to over thirty-seven countries on five continents; trekking through the Amazon rainforest, flying low over glaciers and sailing through icebergs in Greenland, piloting a helicopter and going in a microlite plane, many ski holidays in Europe and North America, numerous coral reef snorkelling holidays in the Red Sea, Caribbean and Indian Ocean; plus the numerous homes where I have lived in London and the English countryside – all in just twenty two years! My health, many assets and intellectual attributes, with which I believe I have been truly 'blessed', are also high on the list.

My practices of prayer, meditation and helping others similarly afflicted, along with my studies of world religions, philosophy, geology, natural history and astronomy have broadened my mind and in the process have helped me 'find myself'; a being that I very much like and had completely lost. I believe they were the tools that nourished my soul back to life. Today I try hard to live by the moral values I was taught as a child, though I do not always succeed: *fear* and *self-centredness* still win some battles but never the war. I do my best and mostly I do not beat myself up when I stumble or fall. To say the least, my gratitude list has helped me many times get my thinking out of the doldrums towards which my mind had a natural knack of gravitating. I have been blessed with the gifts of faith, love and freedom that I believe every human being seeks. Net result: today I have much self-worth, but this can still be sent flying like dandelion seeds blown in the wind when I am tired and am not in the best of spiritual conditions. Hence I need to keep my spiritual level topped up at all times: unlike my former spirit level!

So after sobriety, the greatest gift I was given at this stage of my recovery was a growing belief that a *power greater than myself had* always looked after me.

By now my wife and I were quite well off: we were still amply supported by her father and I had quite a good income, honestly arrived at, from stock-broking. I had come to understand that whatever I had of a material nature was not as important as following the spiritual path I was on, nor was my recovery from alcoholism dependent upon how much money I had. I also knew at a very deep level that just one drink or drug would set off a chain reaction over which I would have no control and everything I now had would be lost forever. I realised, too, that if it came from God *it had to be free and available to everyone, anywhere in the world.* Lastly, I grasped that only I could apply the actions for my much-needed, continuing spiritual growth and for this, God would always provide all of the necessary tools.

To improve my spiritual development further I started to

attend our local Hampstead church regularly. Here I met the Reverend Gerry Moate, its newly-appointed vicar. I will never forget what Gerry did for me, and his role in guiding me at this time. He was always kind and patient with me, spending hours sharing experiences of his life before he became a clergyman; some of which were so helpful to my accepting the sins of my own past as to endear him to me forever: not that he had ever done anything as terribly wrong as I had!

After one of our meetings he said, "There is a church in the City that has a service every Tuesday lunchtime that I would like to take you to."

We went there together the following week. It was very crowded. There were many ushers, all very helpful and exceptionally polite. I discovered that due to the church's popularity another service followed immediately after; in total, I was told, about 1,000 people attended each week. It was the first time in my life that I had encountered such enthusiasm for religion, especially Christianity, which I had understood to be waning in most parts of Britain.

The church was St Margaret's, Lothbury, and it was here that I first heard about John Collins, vicar of Holy Trinity, Brompton - 'HTB'. Gerry suggested I contact him to ask if he and I could meet. I rang, and he said he would be delighted to see me the following Tuesday and invited me to his home for tea.

John was fantastically kind as well. We met every week for many months at his home in South Kensington on Tuesday evenings straight after I finished work. I would talk about my history of alcohol and drug abuse and where it had taken me to in life; I dotted the 'i's and crossed the 't's over the most sordid aspects, knowing that honesty was from now on my only way forward. He never once blanched, judged me or put me down. His time freely given I will remember for as long as I live. Sometimes we would discuss passages from the bible but mostly it was free and easy with no agenda. He also talked about the life of Christ and what it meant to him: he never once tried to convert me. He even let me bring my wife to meet him and his wife for tea which I considered a most hospitable thing to do given their immensely busy lives – at this time I still did not think I was worthy of such friendship and hospitality.

What impressed me most about John was something I found out several years later. I had no idea at the time of the stature of 'HTB' or its role in the creation of the worldwide acclaimed 'Alpha' course. Never did he try to persuade me to attend 'HTB' or even to take the course. It was as if he knew I was on my own spiritual path and that he should let my 'Higher Power' guide me; after all, it had done pretty well so far!

Some time later I did attend three 'HTB' services taken by Sandy Millar and I also met their renowned preacher, Nicky Gumble. I could see why they were so popular but I found at that time on my journey their way did not seem quite right for me, and John, I guess, had realised this may be the case too.

A few years further on I heard about one of HTB's well-known supporters, Jackie Pullinger, when I saw a documentary about her on television called 'Chasing the Dragon'. Jackie is famous for her work in Hong Kong with heroin and opium addicts. In 1993 I visited her centre, The

Hang Fook Camp, which used to be in the infamous 'walled city', home to the notorious Hong Kong Triad gangs based there: probably the most dangerous place on earth to be alone at night at that time.

When Jackie had first gone to Hong Kong; alone as a young woman in her twenties, she had lived and worked with the worst of the addicts, criminals and prostitutes. She did not speak a word of Cantonese, the local Chinese dialect, and Christianity was the last thing on the minds of those who lived there. Due to her own deep faith in God and living life through Jesus Christ she had put up with the conditions until such time as the 'walled city' was knocked down in the early nineties. By then, using the simple but effective formula of love and prayer, she had shown many of the most hardened drug addicts, gangsters and hookers how to kick their habit and also how to change their lives.

When I visited her clinic I was able to see at first hand the wonders of the work she, or 'God' as I now better understood Him, had done. An account of her ministry appears both in her book: *Chasing the Dragon* and in *Crack in the Wall,* both of which are magnificent accounts of both faith and courage. And if any reader has any doubts as to the results of her teachings or her amazing story, they too can visit her just as I did.

Once I had been there and studied her work, I realised the results of her endeavours could not be refuted as she only had successes with anyone that had followed her seemingly divinely-inspired directions. There were no failures: all of which helped add to my growing belief in God.

So as a result of my first-hand experiences in London, Hong

Kong and other parts of the British Isles, I had been able to see how many thousands of alcoholics and drug addicts had found freedom from their addictions by praying to "a Power greater than themselves". And as I understood it, there were actually millions who had taken the same approach and were all recovered, too, right across the world. This helped me come to believe that there is a wondrous healing force available to all mankind that resides in the silent, invisible universe. When I remember this, I can apply it to my life and remember that *It* is with me at all times too.

In addition, faith helped me develop self-confidence. I knew that if I was accepted by church leaders *and their God,* it was likely I could be accepted by anyone. After all, my past had introduced me to some very interesting, highly sceptical people and they had accepted me! This helped my self-esteem develop further, as I was now doing business with people whom I would have been afraid even to talk to in recent, by-gone years: Chairmen and Chief Executives of public companies, The City's major institutional fund managers, analysts, lawyers and accountants, and so forth. As my confidence grew, and with advice from my sponsor, I even told some of these over lunches, when it seemed appropriate, that I had once had an alcohol and drug problem; none of them batted an eyelid and often told me of relatives of theirs or colleagues who had had similar problems. The support I always got was fantastic and of course it meant I could be open and not hide these essential facts about myself.

***

My faith in God was always quite tenuous and I needed substantial reassurance to be certain He, She or It really did exist. Needless to say, I got what I needed in the most unexpected forms; sometimes in big blasts but mostly in the form of simple coincidences, for none of which I was responsible. This, I found, was always the case on *my journey into light.*

I was less than a year sober and driving home from meeting some sober alcoholic friends in Chelsea. For some reason unbeknown to me, I had gradually, over several days, fallen into the most horrendous state of depression. My mind had become completely enveloped in a despairing hopelessness as to what future life held in store for me. It had been so surreptitious in its approach that I had not always been aware of where it was leading; sometimes I was in the midst of it and at others I was teetering on its brink. Tonight I was right at the bottom of the blackest hole I had ever been in. Every direction I looked the outlook ranged from bleak to sheer bloody awful, the drop looked perpendicular and there was nothing I seemed able to do about it.

I kept asking myself, "What is the point of being alive? I am going nowhere fast and there is no way out. I cannot even take drugs or alcohol any more."

Needless to say, I was close to the jumping off point, but I also knew that any form of mood- altering substance would only make matters far worse. There was nothing I could do!

By this time I had learned one of AA's best-loved prayers, one I was currently repeating to myself over and over again as I drove up the Edgware Road on the grimmest night of my life.

I kept saying to myself and out loud,

"God grant me the serenity to accept the things I cannot change,
Courage to change the things I can,
And, Wisdom to know the difference."

I must have said it at least a dozen times.

I had the Peter Gabriel album '*So'* playing in the background, though I was not aware I was listening to it. All at once the words of his classic song, sung with Kate Bush, caught my ear: *Don't Give Up!*

I will never forget the healing impact these words had on me:

Don't give up, you know it's never been easy. P-l-e-a-s-e don't give up!

These lines were repeated many times and as I subconsciously absorbed their meaning my depression started to lift. By the time I reached home ten minutes later I felt totally different. I knew I was safe again, that the future would only get better from here on: it did, and it always has.

Over the next fifteen years I had similar depressions, but none lasted as long or was ever quite so awful. On each occasion, horrible as they were when they occurred, I somehow knew they would pass, and that was always the case. A few 'serenity' prayers, and some time later, I would be out the other side in bright sunshine again: it was like I had peeled off another layer of my wretched past which had needed weeding to let more of the bright light in.

I was told, 'There is no growth without pain', and as a result of my experiences, I can ruefully vouch for that too! Today I am convinced that all my painful episodes were necessary and 'provided' to help develop my faith; this way I always had to apply spiritual tools to pull me through; and as they say, 'practice makes perfect'. So I believe that was what my Higher Power had in store, though He always went without checking with me first!

In the next two years an extraordinary trail of coincidences entered my life. Most of them I cannot remember, but at the time they each helped to reinforce my often shaky belief that a 'Higher Power' was now taking care of me. They happened almost every day and as I still had the expression 'there are no coincidences, it's just God's way of revealing Himself' resonating in my ear, I needed no debate as to their authenticity. Whether my interpretation was right or wrong did not matter, to me it was 100% right as I knew I was the only one on my precise path and this was the way in which God had chosen to reveal Himself to me. I also knew no one else had arrived at the start of their journey in quite the same way as I had, which helped prevent me questioning the spiritual journeys of my peers.

From my perspective the most remarkable coincidence took place one Friday night on my way to a dinner party at a friend, Steve's place. My wife and I had just left home by car and she asked me what I was planning to do the next day. I had not got a clue. Suddenly I remembered it was the FA Cup Final, Wimbledon were playing Liverpool.

I replied, "I'm probably going to watch the Cup Final in the afternoon." I wanted to give the impression I was busy in case she was considering other plans for me! She did not reply.

At this time I often occupied my mind whilst driving looking at car registration numbers; I would figure out words or expressions from the combinations of their letters. Almost as the words spilled out of my mouth the very next car had as its first three letters, 'WNR'.

I immediately translated this as 'WiNneR'.

The next car had the letters, 'WMN' – WiMbledoN! I could not believe it!
And when the very next one was, 'WMD'; again WiMbleDon…

…and the one immediately after was 'WNS' -- 'WiNS'…

…I almost drove onto the pavement!!

I sat almost bolt upright, afraid to say anything. I knew from my considerable experience of studying British car number plates that each of these combinations was unusual, and to have them appear on consecutive cars was bordering on the impossible; yet there they were, one immediately after the other with no gaps in between.

I knew Wimbledon were the biggest outsiders to win for years and I wondered if this truly was a divinely inspired message. I said nothing at dinner, believing everyone would think I was stark raving mad if I relayed my story. I did not even tell my wife until we were on our way home. She was totally nonplussed so I quickly dropped the subject.

Next day I awoke wondering what to do. I was a little nervous and excited but determined to put a big bet on

Wimbledon to win. I was struggling to determine how much when I went into a betting shop in Marlowes Road, Kensington. The odds on their blackboard enticed me to bet even more!

My old Herefordshire Constabulary police number was 114, and Wimbledon were 11/4 against. I immediately knew how much to put on!

Less than an hour later I was watching the match at Campden Hill Tennis Club with some friends: again I said nothing. When Wimbledon scored I nearly fell off my chair with excitement. I spent every second of the rest of the match with my nerves on edge and the final few minutes seeming to drag on forever. Then the final whistle blew and Wimbledon had won! I leapt with joy and I was immediately off to the betting shop to collect my winnings; wishing, of course, I had put much more on.

Whether or not these coincidences were divinely inspired I will never know. However, what I do know is that I would not have put money on the outcome of the match, or been much better off as a result, if I had not taken the view that it was. Today I have no qualms with anyone thinking my actions were insane and I know I would do the same again should a similar string of coincidences arise in my life; though this time I might consider putting a whole lot more on the outcome!

Steve, the party-giver, loved to gamble on the stock market. The next time I saw him I shared my experience with him. He said, "I wish you had told me! I would have bet my shirt on Wimbledon, it would be like receiving inside information in the stock market."

"Hmm!" I thought, "Let's just hope it happens again."

At the time my faith was still up and down but strengthening all the time. I had started to meditate and read spiritual books every morning and at other times during the day and at night as well. Almost out-of-the-blue I started to see 'crosses': the same as those used as the symbol in Christianity. Even as I write this I imagine readers will think I was going potty! But that *is* what happened. I could be almost anywhere and whenever I felt fear or anger creeping into my emotions I would see a cross. The 'cross' was usually the cross-panelling in a wooden door, the wooden intersections of a window frame or the joins in a ceiling, floor and wall tiles. Never did I try to create them; they would just appear and always at times when I needed my faith strengthened. I found them a great comfort at many times and they gave me the courage to go on; especially when I was pursuing something I was fearful about, such as operations without anaesthetic in hospitals: which I had to do for three endoscopies. Today I still see them but now they are just part of my everyday life, but always reassuring.

I remember the first time I flew in an aeroplane in recovery. I had always been terrified of flying and as I mounted the steps to the plane my fears came flooding back to me. Immediately I started repeating the serenity prayer. Suddenly there, by the passenger door, where sheets of metal joined, was the perfect Christian style cross. Immediately my fears evaporated for I knew God was on board already. On the hundreds of occasions I have flown since not once has my fear of flying returned with the force it once had.

There were two occasions when I had the feeling my Higher

Power had arrived at my destination before me. The first was on a visit to Dallas. Immediately on disembarking from the plane there was a huge sign, "AA welcomes you to the U.S.A.": 'yes', I did feel welcome. The second was on a holiday to Brazil with my wife. I was only three years sober and still nervous about being away from my regular London surroundings. We were staying in Manaus, the old Portuguese city in the heart of the Amazon jungle. Nerves jangling, as I knew there were no AA meetings there, I went outside the airport concourse to get a taxi. Immediately my mind was at ease: every car had the registration letters 'AA'! I knew I was as safe here in this isolated spot as any other I could visit on the planet.

Again I do not care what other people think. This is my story and for me this is what has worked. Today I am a great believer in the old adage, 'if it works don't fix it.'

It was shortly after this that I was given my biggest spiritual boost of all.

Chapter 9

A NEW WAY OF LIFE

When I was in my early teens my father watched me nearly drown. He stood on a bridge helplessly looking down into the River Wye in Wales in a state of sheer panic, unable to do anything to help me. On this occasion some friends swimming nearby rescued me. I was one of three children and my eldest sister had already died from a fall several years earlier, so the fear at this time in my father must have been horrendous.

Nearly thirty years later, in my second year of recovery from alcoholism, I dreamt about this drowning incident. This time I was lifted from the water and slowly rose upwards, following about five strides behind a figure wearing a white full-length gown, who when he turned and looked at me, was the image of the most commonly-held impression of Jesus Christ – long, dark flowing hair, gentle face, beard and so on. After we had risen about fifty metres, I was gently set down on earth again, together with several suitcases I was carrying.

At that point I awoke. Running through my sleepy mind were the words of the Leonard Cohen song *Suzanne*:

And Jesus was a sailor when He walked upon the water,
And when He knew for certain only drowning men could see Him.

After subconsciously repeating these lines several times, I got up and went downstairs to the kitchen. For a few minutes

I stood motionless, gazing through a window at the night sky, playing over and over again these same words in my head: then I remembered another line and this one had me fully awake immediately,

He let the river answer that He'd always been your lover.

Instantly my mind was fully concentrated on these incredible 'messages'. In much amazement I quickly concluded that here was the evidence of Providence I had always sought: I had my own Guardian Angel looking after me, and that had been the case even in my darkest hours. I could hardly believe it, but believe it I did: these were facts and although they emanated from the surreal, the 'I' in me had not created them, they were as real as the leaves on the trees and the birds of the air I so much loved; I felt good about them and that was all I needed to know.

As I pondered further, I realized the method of revelation was right in line with the *modus operandi* I knew I could expect from the Father I had so recently come to believe in, subtle but also obvious, now that I knew what to look for. His fingerprints I had started to see were everywhere but close- mindedness, arrogance and not knowing how or where to look had dogged my every step before. Now open-mindedness, a little humility and an honest desire to try to find God had led me to this point on my spiritual path; our game of hide and seek was over.

I have never forgotten either the dream or the words of the song and have often recalled them since at low times in my life. I saw that I had had a gradual spiritual awakening and I had also

been blessed with a profound spiritual experience. I came to believe that this was the easy-to-see start of my resurrection and that I was then, and have been ever since, looked after by my Heavenly Father.

Around the same time as my drowning incident, in a school Latin lesson, I gently threw a pair of dividers at a female classmate called Ann, whom I was keen on. She shrieked with pain as the point of one end stuck in her thigh. Ann liked another boy, Roger, more than me and this was my way of venting my jealousy, of taking revenge. I was severely reprimanded but that did not stop me pursuing a life where this kind of behavior, followed by much misery as I was punished, was to persist for many years to come.

Although I hated both mental and physical pain, *I could not see it was my behavior that caused all of my problems*. I had always thought that they were caused by other people; how stupid and wrong could I have been?

From the bottom of my self-created hellhole has emerged a new life full of hope for the future, much peace in the present and happiness akin to my earliest childhood memories.

I have since come to interpret my dream as the gift of a second chance and that the suitcases contained all the experiences from my former life. My being put back on earth again meant I was given all I would need to live out the rest of my life and at the same time I was to pass on this message to others: mostly no-hoper alcoholics and addicts. Though what the suitcases really contained I do not know, nor will I ever know if my dream interpretation was correct: but what does that matter, as I reflect upon the impact it had on me and the life I have been blessed with today?

Looking back further, I now believe that my life had always been one of preparation for where I am at precisely today. In my first forty-five years I had spent time in Northern Ireland, South Africa, India, Israel, the USA and Yugoslavia, and when the racial, ethnic or religious troubles arose in each, I found it useful to reflect from first-hand experience upon those things that I had witnessed in each of these countries.

The time I had spent working in the British Police's Criminal Investigation Department gave me insights into legal and criminal procedure, which I could also apply to my reflections.

Adding this experience to my more recent studies of the teachings and practices of the world's major religions and philosophy; plus what I had learned from my examinations of geology, astronomy, natural history and science, helped me come to believe that there is a presiding, all- powerful Creator of all that is, ever has been and always will be. And even though some of His methods did not make sense to me, I came to realize His plan must be that one day all mankind will live in peace and harmony: though how we get to that time is for Him to decide, not me!

As I had never had worldly views before, and certainly none of a positive kind, I was somewhat surprised as to my ability to arrive at such a philosophical conclusion. A smile still comes over my face every time I muse on the progress I had made and that a spiritual awakening should have happened to a bum like me.

Since embarking upon my new way of life it has always seemed as though I was being led rather than charting my own course – not 'my way' any more. Either I would be introduced to a new book or guru, or I would receive some new idea or revelation to help my understanding. These revelations would often come from a totally unexpected source. Therefore I learned to listen to everyone I met just in case they were the next link in my spiritual chain of development. The sources were people I talked to at dinner and cocktail parties, new and old friends, airline and train passengers, taxi drivers and others who briefly entered my life. It seemed as though as long as I stayed open-minded and was aware I was being led, the instructions would naturally flow.

Often the new facts of nature I unearthed, and my interpretations, seemed quite bizarre, yet always they were original to me and exquisitely timed: whilst sometimes they reinforced what I already knew. I recalled again the expression, *When the student is ready the teacher appears:* every encounter seemed to happen at precisely the right time, not a second too soon, or a minute, hour or day too late!

One of the most astonishing of these occurred on a plane flight between Denver and Los Angeles. I was in the middle of a ski holiday in Breckenridge and just before leaving England I had a read a Deepak Chopra book that made references to Merlin the magician. Due to my Welsh heritage and enthusiasm for spiritual enlightenment, I had made endeavours in local bookshops and libraries to study Merlin's wizardry further. I had not found it easy and come up with very little.

I was half way through the flight when lunch was served. Many times in the recent past I had used this time to start a conversation with my fellow passenger. I had glanced at the man sitting next to me once or twice but not found him too inspiring; he seemed to be reading a children's book!

After debating in my head whether to speak or not I finally said, "Hello. I was wondering what you are reading?"

He laughed and closed the book so that I could not see the cover. He said with embarrassment, "It's a children's book. As I was leaving home I just grabbed it as I went through the door. It's one of my twelve-year-old son's school reading books."

I said, "Is it any good?"

Again he laughed and said, "Yes, it's quite interesting. It's the story of a magician called Merlin." I could not believe it!

I said, "You may not believe this but I have been hunting high and low in England for information about the history of Merlin and not come up with anything worthwhile. Do you mind if I have a look at it?"

It transpired his son's book contained all I needed to know about Merlin. And the moral to this story: *Never judge a book by its cover!*

Since then I have seldom held back in opening conversations with strangers who have been put in my path: though one or two taxi drivers were not quite as enlightening as my American co-passenger!

This meeting was just one of many instances along these lines. There were numerous others, all of which added to my spiritual growth. One of the most interesting was meeting Jo, who gave me numerous similar introductions to authors and an anthologist with whose works I was unfamiliar.

Jo had been on her own spiritual path for many years and was a great fan of Carlos Castaneda and Joseph Campbell. But it was when she introduced me to Dostoyevsky's *Diary of a Writer* that my spiritual journey went forward in leaps and bounds. Reading his dream about 'paradise' where everyone lived in harmony, after my own dream experience, and my already being a fan of Sir Thomas Mores' idea of 'Utopia', left me with an almost certain belief that such a 'paradise' or 'Utopia' was precisely what God has in store for the people of planet Earth. What other divine purpose could there be? I reasoned.

One other major occurrence had a profound influence on my early spiritual development. When I had been drug-free for about two years I went on a two-week European business trip to Paris, Rome, Athens, Vienna, Geneva, Zurich, Lugano and Brussels. In the middle weekend I decided to make a social visit to Venice rather than return to London. I had visited Venice once, seven years previously, with a friend Julia, on the first of my many attempts to stop drinking. This failed miserably and I remembered little of the weekend except that much of it was yet another unhappy drunken experience.

Julia was a doctor's daughter and I thought her father's medicinal influence might have rubbed off on her, and so help me find the strength I needed to quit the by now dreaded booze. Little did I realize then that no other person could help solve my addiction problem: it had to be an inside job. I had to find the willingness and strength within me to conquer my overwhelming need for alcohol and drugs.

As my plane was circling over the Venetian lagoon before landing, I got out my previous trips' Venice guide. I had not opened it since that time, and inside, much to my surprise, I found an old grey postcard, which was actually a photograph of the inside of a church: it was called Santa Maria dei Miracoli.

As soon as I read its name I became excited; I knew almost for certain that something special had happened to me there: I assumed the translation must be 'The Church of St Mary of the Miracle'.

Immediately after breakfast the next day, I found my way to the church and total recall came flooding back. I remembered how my friend had become angry with me because I had got drunk the previous night in Harry's bar. She had left me sitting alone on the church steps. Wallowing in self-pity, I had started to sob. As my despair enveloped me more and more, I had lain down and ended up crying uncontrollably - realizing for the first time in my life that I was completely beaten by alcohol and I was inevitably going to die. I lay there for some fifteen minutes as this realization grew deeper and deeper. I eventually got up, caught up with my friend, apologized, and spent the rest of the weekend drowning my sorrows and asking her to forgive my pathetic disposition.

Little did I know then that my *cri de coeur* was being heard and would be answered in full several years later, but that in the interim my situation would get many times worse. Indeed, that my downhill progression had scarce begun, for in front of me lay the worst five years of living that I could ever have imagined!

But that 'Santa Maria' experience was then, and this was now. I was recapping on other instances where the name 'Maria' had transpired to influence me. I recalled my encounter with the prostitute who called herself 'Santa Maria', and that on this, the second night I had met her, I was wining and dining with the one 'true love' of my life also, Maria. I then recalled how on my earlier skiing holiday to Switzerland, when I drank on *Antabuse* for the first time, that it was a *'Virgin Mary'* I had been sipping! Although these were little things, they all added to my belief that I was being divinely led.

Although my dream and these incidents did not provide me with a clear-cut certainty that I had my very own Guardian Angel, they were sufficient for me to think that maybe I had. Their timing, and the way they had built up, coupled with my many other coincidences and seeing crosses, were enough to convince me this actually was the case.

I concluded, therefore, through sorting out my past, making amends where necessary: prayer, meditation, spiritual reading and service to others, I had found a way of life that was preferable to any I had known before or had witnessed elsewhere. I could also see that each spiritual journey is individual and only relevant to the person on it, but that each of us can climb aboard at any time we are willing to plead for help. I have seen this in many others, who, after faltering steps to begin with, once on board have had profound spiritual awakenings too. So as I had seen with Jacky Pullinger's opium addicts in Hong Kong, I now had sufficient proof to believe that anyone who wishes to conquer their addiction to any form of drug whatsoever only has to pray for help from the bottom of their heart and **It** always materialises.

****

In 2016 I made my fourth and fifth visits to Morocco. When I discovered they had no AA or NA for their million plus drug addicts and had the worst drug problems of the thirty four countries I had visited in my recovery, in January 2017 I packed my bags and moved there. Though there is a long way to go to get these fellowships established, it was and still is the best thing I have ever done.

'Surviving Addictions' is dedicated to drug addicts, alcoholics and their families everywhere. But I do have a special soft spot for Morocco's.

Chapter 10

A Never Ending Story.
The Best was yet to come.

If I could have written a script for the way my life would pan out going forward from the day I quit all drugs, I would have short-changed myself thousands of times.

The best years of my life began when I was forty and have got better ever since; now, thirty five years later, when I look back I see that every year progressed positively, and my most recent yesterdays' have also kept getting better.

If someone had told me on 1st August 1985 when I was three days abstinent that the rest of my life would be beyond my wildest dreams, I would have thought they were insane. At that time I would have given anything just to stay off mood altering drugs until I died, because that would have been enough.

Working again I thought would be out of the question, becoming a father, a respectable human being, mergers and acquisitions adviser to the pharmaceutical industry, traveling to five continents, living in Morocco, spending months in the Caribbean, two years in Europe, twenty years as an author, are just some of things I could never have imagined happening to an out-of-work alcoholic and drug addicted bum like me.

But they did and that is where I am at today: a seventy five year old man full of gratitude and peace of mind who has many friends, and most all, I love myself.

The reason I wrote 'Surviving Addictions' was to give addicts and alcoholics hope that they too can recover. The aim of this last chapter is to demonstrate what can be achieved by anyone who applies a 12 Step Programme of Recovery in their lives and a directory of those that are available.

I know I am not special, but because I was so desperate to change, to the best of my ability I followed the suggestions my Alcoholics Anonymous sponsors passed on to me. So, if you find a programme that is right for you, something similar to my experience may well happen and a life beyond your wildest dreams unfold. This is my story and what happened to me.

How do you go from being a chronic alcoholic and drug addict living in London, who goes to Morocco to start a business importing cans of sardines in 1984, to becoming a man who has been clean and sober thirty five years, a business development adviser to the pharmaceutical industry, and then goes to live there to help their one million drug addicts recover?

My name is Jack Llewelyn. I am a former drug addict and alcoholic and that is what happened to me.

I first set foot on Moroccan soil when my soon-to-be entrepreneurial father-in-law sent me there to start an import business in tinned fish! At the time I was a no-good bum; so the last thing he wanted was that his Jewish 'princess' daughter marry anyone other than a respectable human being.

What no one could have anticipated was that this would be the start of a global adventure involving legal and illegal drugs, Big Pharma, mafias and Government skullduggery in many countries, on a scale impossible to imagine.

Although nothing significant happened on that first trip - except that I drank a lot of alcohol and took a lot of drugs - it laid the foundation for what was to happen to me years later.

In that time, I went from being an out-of-work chronic alcoholic, drug addict and criminal, to a man people respected and listened to. While Morocco went from cannabis being available all over Europe, to its citizens being responsible for some of the worst crimes in the world. I was to discover this was influenced by its loose policies regarding drugs - especially those relating to Karkoubi, its 'Drug of Mass Destruction' - and almost non-existent success treating drug addiction and alcoholism.

I realised it means that unless Morocco changes its drug laws and policies which cause, or add to the problems, worse will follow. On the other hand, if it makes the right changes, it will give it the potential to become a role model for other countries. And as such role-models already exist, there is no excuse for Morocco's king and government not to apply the methods these countries adopted to sort out their mega drug problems.

The second time I went to Morocco was on holiday to Marrakesh. After going to the two weekly AA meetings there, I was surprised that none of the members were Moroccan and the meetings were only in French and English, not Arabic.

The third time I went was for a weekend to Ceuta, the tiny controversial Spanish territory in northern Morocco: the Spanish claim it is theirs - just as the British do in Spain with regard Gibraltar - while as Morocco borders it on every side, except the one on the Mediterranean Sea, they insist it is theirs.

This, and a similar Spanish enclave in Melilla, 250 kilometres away on the same Moroccan coast is equally controversial. Everyday thousands of Moroccan "cargo women" risk their lives weighed down with heavy bundles as they cross the border. They live under the burden of exploitation, with their health and lives at risk. This causes stampedes and has a history of deaths, and until recently, nothing was done about it. The sight of this was nothing but horrendous and inhumane.

All of this is due to the extremes of poverty in this region of Morocco, caused by both Spanish claimed cities being magnets for thousands of traders and menial workers who cross the border from Morocco to earn a living. It meant that what I discovered appalled me, but it also helped me understand the reality of Morocco's deeply imbedded problems.

But, it was the fourth time I went to Morocco that changed my life forever. I had bought a motor home, aiming to tour France, Spain and Portugal to do research for a book I was writing about the worldwide success of AA, Narcotics Anonymous (NA), Alanon and Nar-Anon which specialise in helping families of those afflicted by alcoholism and drug addiction.

Travelling between Seville and Estepona in southern Spain regularly in 2016, I saw signs; *'Tickets Tarifa - Tangier.'* I had never been to Tangier, and given its past reputation, I thought it would be romantic to visit. With no plans for the following weekend, I booked a ferry and made a reservation at the boutique hotel, La Maison Blanche in Tangier's Kasbah. I chose it because the advertising said its owner spoke English and was an expert guide to the city.

Within twenty-four hours of arriving, I started to believe destiny had taken a hand: by the time I left the following Monday, I was convinced it had.

Not only did I keep meeting the right people to convince me serendipity was on the case, but my background and personal circumstances meant I was in the perfect position to try to help the many drug addicts and alcoholics who lived there. (Though in my youth I had always been a coward, afraid of the dark and personal injury. If I had thought about it from that angle, I would not have returned to live there on my own!)

On the ferry back to Tarifa, I reflected on my twenty-year history taking pharmaceutical drugs prescribed by doctors to arrest my twenty five years descent into chronic alcoholism. I thought about my recovery from addiction to all drugs, and similar time working as a business development adviser to the pharmaceutical industry.

When I put these together and added them to my former friendship with Arthur Sackler of Purdue pharmaceuticals, famous for being fined $600,000,000 for mislabeling their drug substitute opiate product, Oxycontin, I knew I had to try to do something. (The Sackler family are the owners of Purdue and Arthur was one of its founders).

But what could one man on his own do? Especially, someone who did not speak Arabic, only English and a little French.

First, I thought of my financial and personal circumstances, and as this developed, I began to know what I believed I must do. Go back to Tangier, find an interpreter and try to establish AA, NA, Alanon and Nar-Anon meetings in Arabic to help Morocco's 1,000,000 drug addicts and their families.

To see if it made sense, I contacted NA and AA's World Services in Los Angeles and New York. They had the experience of establishing their fellowships 12 Step programmes in nearly 200 countries in 80 languages, and more than 3,500,000 people with a variety of addictions have used them to recover in less than eighty years. And all this was achieved by word of mouth, minimal advertising, and often little or no support from governments and the medical profession.

Both organisations answered saying their programmes were available in Arabic and recovery from addiction in the Middle East's Islamic countries was good. In Iran, for example I discovered NA has 400,000 former opium addicts in recovery and 22,500 NA meetings a week. Which is almost as many as in North America where it had started in California forty years earlier.

Based on this information, I made a second visit to Tangier two weeks later. Each fellowships' advice was for me to meet medical professionals. So, this time my aim was to discuss the situation with as many doctors as possible.

I booked into the El Minzha hotel; famous for being the hotel of choice for film stars and personalities from the arts. It was also recommended by an NA friend in the music business who honeymooned there. My reason for choosing it though was because it is central, and walking around the town from there, especially in the evening, I would feel relatively safe. I had found it scary being on my own at night in parts of the Kasbah the last time I was there. The streets were narrow, the lighting poor and the people I saw frightened me.

After breakfast in the first morning, I asked at reception for an English-speaking doctor and made an appointment to meet him. After answering the surgery door, the receptionist told me to sit in the hall, not in the waiting room where there were a number of patients. A few minutes later I was telling the doctor, Allal Abadi, my purpose for being in Tangier and asked if he could help. I also told him I planned to return in January to live there. This was in December 2016.

Today, I am extremely grateful for what happened as the result. At the time I had no idea where it would lead to and was skeptical I was doing the right thing. Dr Abadi said he was on the same wavelength and to leave it with him and come back in the afternoon. So, a few hours later I returned.

In that time this good man had contacted a doctor friend who had an apartment I could rent at a reasonable price on the outskirts of the city. He would also provide a driver and a guard at night. Most importantly he said that between them they knew many medical professionals, not only in Tangier but the whole of Morocco, and would make as many introductions as possible.

The next few days I spent finding out as much as I could about the drug situation in Tangier. I talked to as many people as possible - especially pharmacists, doctors and young people in cafes. I quickly came to realise that the drug problem there was worse there than in any of the thirty-four countries on five continents I had visited since I quit drugs in 1985.

Some of the most disheartening facts of all was the frequent sight of homeless young children addicted to sniffing solvents from plastic bags and women in rags sitting on pavements begging for money to feed their families, while their fathers and husbands sat in cafes drinking tea and smoking!

Equally disheartening was the fact that Morocco's doctor's and psychiatrists do not treat drug addiction and alcoholism as diseases. Instead they prescribe a range of strong, addictive, substitute pharmaceutical drugs to such sufferers. From personal experience I knew this can only ever be a temporary fix, because in almost every instance the addict or alcoholic continues using their usual drug or goes back to them. The net result is that they have an even bigger addiction problem. Withdrawal from such a drug combination is far more dangerous, and invariably needs medically supervised detoxification in a hospital or treatment facility. This is at a financially vast expense to society, and as there is no effective after-care for addicts in Morocco, the problems have only ever spiraled downward.

Of everything I found that was bad about Morocco's problems with drugs, there was one issue I had never encountered before; this was when I was told about an exclusive drug to Morocco called Karkoubi.

From its description, I assumed it was a mood-altering illegal drug similar to K2 or Spice, a form of 'synthetic marijuana.' But the more I found out, the more I realised it was probably the most dangerous drug ever created, and this appeared to be the intention of its makers, dealers and users. The following internet definition explains everything:

'Karkoubi is a 'Rambo' type drug that is everywhere in Morocco. It is so cheap it is called 'the drug of the poor.' As users get to believe they are invincible, it is known for its violent side effects, and is the leading cause of crime among young Moroccans. Statistics show that 80% of police arrests are karboubi related; 5% of Moroccans have taken it in Casablanca alone, while 45% of young people between 12 and 35 say they have used it. It is commonly referred to as Morocco's 'drug of mass destruction.''

Taking in this information was bad enough but worse was to follow. In other internet articles I read that young people under the influence of Karkoubi are easy to radicalise into jihadism, and given that many perpetrators of the world's terrorist attacks are Moroccan, including those in Barcelona, London, Madrid, Paris, Brussels and America's 9/11, it made me wonder if Karkoubi had a direct link to some, or all, of these.

It did not take me long to come to believe that directly or indirectly Karkoubi did have a connection and that the world was unaware of it.

To say I was disturbed would be an understatement. The more I found out, the worse it got, and the more I wondered if there was anything I could do to help; especially because by then I knew Morocco's drug problems are very, very deep.

As one of my favourite expressions is, 'out of little acorns, big oak trees grow', when I returned to live in Tangier on January 10th, 2017, I tried to keep this in mind. I had no plan as to how long I would stay. It would depend on how my endeavours to help the Kingdom of Morocco's drug addicts progressed.

In the end I stayed a year in Tangier, followed by six months in Casablanca. In between, and regularly since, I made numerous visits to Paris, Madrid, Amsterdam and London, because I discovered in these cities Moroccan men and women members of AA and NA who are in recovery. This gave me hope, as by now I knew recovery from drug addiction in Morocco for its Arabic speaking population was non-existent. Though there were many of its drug addicts and alcoholics its medical profession had parked on drug substitutes to pacify them!

Today, wherever I am, I spend several hours each day helping nurture the seeds I planted with the contacts I made when I lived there and in the aforementioned cities. In the not too distant future, I am hopeful many of them will recover as a result all over Morocco, and this will spread across North Africa to Tunisia, Algeria and Libya, where the situation is equally awful and they speak a similar Arabic dialect.

****

In the time I was in Tangier, the two doctors and I became good friends. Over and over again they guided me whom to meet next. Dr. Abadi also found me the perfect place to have meetings and where to eat what he called 'happy couscous' Friday lunches. This was at the Darna Association, a charitable association for fatherless children that did Moroccan set lunches every day in a lovely little courtyard. It was popular with tourists, and served good Moroccan cuisine at attractive prices.

In April that year I started the first ever AA meeting in Morocco for Moroccans. This was in a room at the Darna which eight people attended. Within nine months more fledgling meetings of NA, AA and Al-Anon started in Casablanca and Rabat. Within eighteen months I had met hundreds of Morocco's doctors, psychiatrists, psychologists and pharmacists in one-on-one meetings, explaining how AA and NA work and the global success each had achieved.

When I took my last flight from Casablanca in September 2018, I knew that I had done all I could to replicate the international success of each country where NA and AA are established. From now on it was up to Moroccans to do the same.

Today, there is a hospital in Casablanca and another in Rabat whose psychiatrists realised the need to establish AA and NA programmes of recovery in Arabic to treat Morocco's alcoholics and drug addicts. There are a handful of French and English speaking meetings in Marrakesh, Agadir and Casablanca catering for foreign nationals who live there or visit. There are also online meetings and literature for both fellowships in Arabic, but these are in Classical Arabic not Moroccan Arabic which is somewhat different, so they will need translating.

But the biggest obstacles to making the changes that are needed lie with Morocco's King, government and medical profession not the translation of the NA and AA programmes. This is because if they don't alter their hypocritical drug laws, unhelpful interpretations of the Qur'an regarding drugs, treat addiction as a disease - thereby not prescribing drug substitutes for addicts and alcoholics - and adjust their attitude to cannabis, their policies will continue to wreak havoc on Morocco's people and societies globally.

This is a tall order. But it is Morocco's humanitarian duty to make such changes. Because it is only by their leaders giving unconditional and sustained support will it cleanse their present archaic system. This means that only the right moves in the right direction will accomplish this. If Morocco does this, it can go from influencing some of the worst drug problems in the world to having some of the best results.

****

12 Step Fellowships.

12-Step programmes are designed to promote emotional well-being for many different conditions, not just abstinence from drugs and alcohol. One of the earliest of these was the Al-Anon programme which is typical of all the others. It is derived from Alcoholics Anonymous for people who live with, or once lived with, one or more alcoholics. Its aim is to help this person learn to cope with the alcoholic, whether he or she is drinking or not.

Some of the principles that help Al-Anon members do this are 'letting go' in the form of detachment, learning to live 'one day at a time', remembering nothing lasts forever, as 'this too shall pass', learning to love themselves by doing what is good for them, as the solution to most problems resides in our own attitudes and behaviour.

12-Step programs emphasise the importance of trusting that even when things seem to be going wrong, there is a deeper, more long-term perspective the individual can look forward to, that 'Every cloud has a silver lining' and there is a power behind all that exists in the universe, which is also applicable to them. In 12-Step Fellowships this is known as a 'Higher Power', or God as they understand Him, She or It. This helps individuals let go of situations and have faith that the world – including theirs - will slowly but surely heal itself.

Several of the steps help individuals create a relationship with a personal 'Higher Power.' Primarily this is done through learning to pray and meditate. But other aspects of the programmes do this as well.

Living 'one day at a time' is one of the most important principles of 12-Step recovery programmes, which in times of difficulty can be broken down into hours or even moments. It is the practice of staying in the present moment which is always possible, because all too often people's minds wander off into fear-ridden unrealities. There are no problems in the present moment, only challenges that can be met one at a time, one moment at a time. Staying in the present keeps fears at bay and converts problems into bite-sized, manageable issues.

Members of 12-Step programmes offer hope to fellow sufferers. They never criticise only identify with similarities based on their own experience. This helps the sufferer realise they are not alone or a bad person, as prior to this they would have been consumed by loneliness, making them feel isolated.

To help an individual apply the programme, they have a sponsor. This is someone of the same sex who had similar experiences before they recovered. Their function is to take the sponsee through the 12 steps of the programme in the same way they did with their sponsor.

Loneliness and past behaviour will have led to low self-esteem, often to the point of hating themselves. Helping others and doing service in the fellowships helps restore this until the person becomes the man or woman they always wanted to be.

The overall result is that whatever the person suffered from will be made better. And if he or she continues to apply the principles their 12-Step programme taught them for the rest of their life, they will go on to live happy, spiritual lives full of purpose that benefits mankind. This means they will learn to love themselves. To someone who has lived in the pits of despair, there is no greater gift than that.

****

12-Step Programme Directory

The following is a summary of 12 Steps of Recovery programmes that are available in at least 175 countries in the world today. They have already helped more than three and a half million men, women and young people recover in at least 80 different languages, cultures and religions, as well as atheists and agnostics. For information about what is available where you live, check on-line directories.

Alcoholics Anonymous has done far more than achieve success with alcoholism. Today it is recognised as having been a great venture in social pioneering which forged a new instrument for social action, a new therapy based on the kinship of common suffering, one having vast potential for the myriad other ills of mankind. As the result, many addiction and other recovery programmes have been born from A.A's. 12 Steps. Each adapted to address a specific problem from a wide range of substance, dependency abuse and emotional issues. Every one of these self-help fellowships employs the same 12 step principles to recover.

Drug Addiction.

Alcoholics Anonymous (AA) and Narcotics Anonymous (NA) programmes of recovery and worldwide success are described in detail in previous chapters.

To make contact with **AA** in one of the countries where it is established, go to its website and look for your countries' contact: **http://www.aa.org/**

NA is also established worldwide. For information, contacts and meetings go to: **http:// www.na.org/**

Cocaine Anonymous (CA), deals with cocaine and crack addiction. **https://www.ca.org/**

Crystal Meth Anonymous (CMA), is a relatively new 12 Step programme for people addicted to crystal meth. Links to its website provide support for family and friends as well. **http://www.crystalmeth.org/**

Marijuana Anonymous (MA), is a fellowship of people who share their experience, strength, and hope with each other that they may solve their common problem and help others to recover from marijuana addiction.
Go to their website for more information: **https://www.marijuana-anonymous.org/**

Nicotine Anonymous is a fellowship of men and women who help each other live nicotine-free lives. They welcome all those seeking freedom from nicotine addiction, including those using cessation programs and nicotine withdrawal aids. The primary purpose of Nicotine Anonymous is to help all those who would like to cease using tobacco and nicotine products in any form. The fellowship offers group support and recovery using the 12 Steps to achieve abstinence from nicotine: **https://www.nicotine-anonymous.org/**

Pills Anonymous (PA), is a fellowship of recovering pill addicts throughout the world who share their experience strength and hope as to how they stopped using pills. **http://pillsanonymous.org/**

Behavioral addictions.

Gambling, crime, food, sex, hoarding, debtors, and work are addressed in fellowships such as:

Clutterers Anonymous, (CLA) is a 12-step recovery program which offers help to people who are overwhelmed by disorder. FAQs, literature, meeting list, and CLA background information are available at; **https://www.clutterersanonymous.org/**

Debtors Anonymous (DA) helps people recover from compulsive debting and under earning. **https://www.debtorsanonymous.org**

Emotions Anonymous, is for recovery from mental and emotional illness and based on the 12 steps of A.A. **https://www. emotionsanonymous.org/**

Food Addicts in Recovery (FA) is an international fellowship of men and women who have experienced difficulties in life as a result of the way they eat and were obsessed with food. They found they needed a 12 step programme of recovery and fellowship of others who shared their problem in order to stop abusing food and a live normal life: **https://www.foodaddicts.org**

Gamblers Anonymous (GA), is a fellowship of men and women who share their experience, strength and hope with each other that they may solve their common problem and help others to recover from a gambling problem. The primary purpose is to stop gambling and help other compulsive gamblers do the same. They are convinced that gamblers of their type are in the grip of a progressive illness. Over any considerable period of time they get worse, never better.

The fellowship is the outgrowth of a chance meeting between two men in 1957. Both had a baffling history of trouble and misery due to an obsession to gamble. They began to meet regularly and as the months passed neither had returned to gambling. Since that time, the fellowship has grown and groups are flourishing in at least 58 countries in the world; many in local languages and dialects.

They concluded from their experience that in order to prevent a relapse it was necessary to bring about certain character changes within themselves. In order to accomplish this, they used for a guide certain spiritual principles that are today utilised by millions of people who are recovering from other addictions. The word spiritual can be said to describe those characteristics of the human mind that represent the highest and finest qualities such as kindness, generosity, honesty and humility. Also, in order to maintain their own abstinence they felt that it was important that they carry the message of hope to other compulsive gamblers. **https://gamblersanonymous.org**

Overeaters Anonymous (OA) No matter what the problem with food, whether it is compulsive over-eating, under-eating, addiction, anorexia, bulimia, binge eating, or over-exercising, OA has a solution. Starting in Los Angeles in 1960, they now have 6,500 groups in more than 75 countries, with a total membership of over 50,000 people. **https://oa.org/**

Sex Addicts Anonymous (SAA), is a 12 step fellowship of recovering addicts that offers a message of hope to anyone who suffers from sex addiction. They are addicts who were powerless over their sexual thoughts and behaviors and preoccupation with sex was causing progressively severe adverse consequences for them, their families, and friends. Despite many failed promises to ourselves and attempts to change, they discovered that they were unable to stop acting out sexually by themselves: **https://saa-recovery.org/**

Sex and Love Addicts Anonymous (SLA), is a twelve-step program for people recovering from sex and love addiction. **www.slaauk.org/**

Sexual Compulsives Anonymous, (SCA) SCA is a 12-Step fellowship, inclusive of all sexual orientations, open to anyone with a desire to recover from sexual compulsion. Our primary purpose is to stay sexually sober and to help others to achieve sexual sobriety. Members are encouraged to develop their own sexual recovery plan, and to define sexual sobriety for themselves. **www.sca-recovery.org/**

Workaholics Anonymous, (W.A.) is a fellowship of individuals who share their experience, strength and hope with each other that they may solve their common problems and help others to recover from workaholism. The only requirement for membership is the desire to stop working compulsively. **www.workaholics-anonymous.org/**

Auxiliary groups for friends and families of alcoholics and addicts, are part of a response to treating addiction as a disease that is enabled by family systems.

Al-Anon is a worldwide fellowship that offers a program of recovery for the families and friends of alcoholics whether or not the alcoholic recognises the existence of a drinking problem or seeks help. **https://al-anon.org**

Alateen is part of the Al-Anon fellowship designed for the younger relatives and friends of alcoholics through the teen years.

Al-Anon and Alateen Family Groups are fellowships of relatives and friends of alcoholics who share their experience, strength, and hope in order to solve their common problems. They believe alcoholism is a family illness and that changed attitudes can aid recovery. They are not allied with any sect, denomination, political entity, organization, or institution; do not engage in any controversy; neither endorse nor oppose any cause. There are no dues for membership. They are self-supporting through our own voluntary contributions.

Their groups have but one purpose: to help families of alcoholics. They do this by practicing the 12 Steps, by welcoming and giving comfort to families of alcoholics, and by giving understanding and encouragement to the alcoholic. The meetings often begin with the suggested Al-Anon/Alateen welcome: "We welcome you to this Al-Anon Family Group and hope you will find in this fellowship the help and friendship we have been privileged to enjoy. We who live, or have lived, with the problem of alcoholism understand as perhaps few others can. We, too, were lonely and frustrated, but in Al-Anon and Alateen we discover that no situation is really hopeless, and that it is possible for us to find contentment, and even happiness, whether the alcoholic is still drinking or not."

Al-Anon was co-founded in 1951, 16 years after the founding of Alcoholics Anonymous by Lois W (wife of A.A. co-founder Bill W) and Anne B.

Alateen, began in California in 1957 when a teenager named Bob joined with five other young people who had been affected by the alcoholism of a family member.

Al-Anon and Alateen meetings are held in 56 countries, in local languages and dialects as well as English. **https://al-anon.org**

Adult Children of Alcoholics/Dysfunctional Families. (ACA) ACA's 12 Step programme was developed to deal with the effects of alcoholism or other family dysfunction, found in such homes. The term "adult child" was originally used to describe adults who grew up in alcoholic homes and who exhibited identifiable traits that reveal past abuse or neglect. Its members have histories of abuse, shame, co-dependency and abandonment found in such dysfunctional homes. Today their groups include adults raised in homes without the presence of alcohol or drugs. Meetings are established in 50 countries and ACA literature is available in 19 languages. **www.adultchildren.org/**

Co-Dependents Anonymous (CoDA), addresses compulsions related to relationships. They have informal self-help groups made up of men and women with a common interest in working through the problems that co-dependency has caused in their lives. CoDA is based on Alcoholics Anonymous 12 Steps of recovery programme and adapted to meet CoDA's purposes. To attend meetings, all you need is the willingness to work at having healthy relationships. This means that all kinds of people attend. Individual members can and do have differing political, religious, cultural, ethnic, and other affiliations, but since these are not relevant to the business of recovery from co-dependency, no comment is made about them. CoDA has approximately 2,000 weekly meetings in 60 countries: there are online and phone meetings as well: **www.coda.org/**

There are more than forty other specialist **12 Step Fellowships** that cover other addictions, emotional and psychological disorders. Details of these can be found on the internet or from medical professionals. There is one for almost everybody who suffers such problems.

Printed in Great Britain
by Amazon

80745476R00139